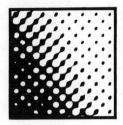

Facing Value Decisions:
Rationale-building for Teachers

Wadsworth Series in Curriculum and Instruction

Series Editor:

Jack R. Fraenkel
San Francisco State University

Published Volumes:

Educational Research: A Guide to the Process
Norman E. Wallen
San Francisco State University

Facing Value Decisions: Rationale-building for Teachers
James Porter Shaver and William Strong
Utah State University

Forthcoming:

Classroom Strategies: Observations and Models
Jane M. Stallings
Stanford Research Institute

For the cover, the designer has chosen an orange and a blue, two bright complementary colors that appear inside the square. In the areas surrounding the square, the two colors are combined in varying amounts to produce colors that become increasingly more neutral toward the center, and increasingly more intense toward the outer border. Orange dots appear to emerge from a blue background in the upper right-hand corner, and vice versa in the lower left-hand corner. The resulting directional flows established by the changing color and intensity in the background represent the complex interrelations of value systems. The simplicity and purity of the orange and blue image inside the square represent the clarity of a rationale built on the careful examination of value systems.

Facing Value Decisions:
Rationale-building for Teachers

James P. Shaver
William Strong

Utah State University

Wadsworth Publishing Company, Inc.
Belmont, California

**This book is for our folks,
who loved and trusted us enough
to value our valuing**

Jim and Bill

Education Editor: Roger S. Peterson
Designer: Ann Wilkinson

© 1976 by Wadsworth Publishing Company, Inc., Belmont, California 94002. All rights reserved. No part of this book may be reproduced, stored in a retrieval system or transcribed, in any form or by any means, electronic, mechanical, photocopying, recording or otherwise, without the prior written permission of the publisher.

ISBN 0-534-00441-5
L. C. Cat. Card No. 75–32231
Printed in the United States of America
1 2 3 4 5 6 7 8 9 10——80 79 78 77 76

Acknowledgments

Page 2, excerpt from "A Christmas Call to Conscience: Do You Hear the Animals Crying?" by Judith Schmidt, published in *Family Weekly*, Dec. 23, 1973, copyright 1973 by Family Weekly, Inc. and used by permission of Family Weekly, Inc.

Page 6, excerpt from *The Nature of the Social Sciences* by Charles Beard, copyright 1934 Charles Scribner's Sons, renewal copyright 1962 William Beard, used by permission of Charles Scribner's Sons.

Page 28, excerpts from *An American Dilemma* by Gunnar Myrdal, *et al.*, copyright 1944 by Harper & Row Publishers, Incorporated, used by permission of Harper & Row, Publishers.

Pages 43, 57, excerpts from *Black on Black* by Chester Himes. Copyright © 1942, 1943, 1944, 1945, 1949, 1973 by Chester Himes. Used by permission of Doubleday & Company, Inc.

Page 45, excerpt from "Supreme Court Hears Arguments in Minority Admissions Case" by Cheryl M. Fields, published in *The Chronicle of Higher Education*, March 4, 1974, used by permission of the publisher.

Page 58, excerpt from *Stride Toward Freedom* by Martin Luther King, Jr., copyright 1958 by Harper & Row, Publishers, Incorporated, used by permission of Harper & Row, Publishers.

(Continued at back of book.)

Contents

Series Foreword

In recent years, "values education" has increasingly been a topic for professional discussion in educational journals, teacher inservice sessions, professional conferences, and college methods courses. Most of this discussion has focused on two areas: (1) the description and defense of various models designed to teach (or teach about) values and the process of valuing; and (2) descriptions of different techniques that a teacher might use to implement one or more of these models in the classroom. Rarely, however, has there been any sort of critical analysis of either models or techniques with regard to underlying ethical premises, and the degree to which either models or techniques are or are not consistent with such premises.

In filling this lack, Professors Shaver and Strong have produced a noteworthy book. They present the reader with their own rationale for values education and identify the ethical premises which underlie this rationale. And they argue persuasively that it is absolutely essential for the teacher to develop his or her own rationale—a rationale that is intellectually defensible yet emotionally satisfying; a rationale that is based on fundamental value assumptions carefully thought out and clearly articulated. Only in this way will the teacher have anything more than a whimsical basis for dealing with values in elementary and secondary school classrooms.

The attainment of this goal—helping and encouraging teachers to develop such a rationale—is one of the authors' central concerns. A second concern—and a major theme of the book—is to help teachers (or anyone else interested) to help students develop a rational foundation for their own values, and learn the skills they will always need to analyze and defend their values rationally. Ideas about ways to achieve both goals abound throughout the book. A particularly exciting feature is a set of value explorations and exercises in which the authors present a variety of activities, vignettes, and provocative questions to help the reader think about values and how to deal with them in the classroom.

This is not a book of methodology, however. Rather, it is intended, in the authors' words, "to start the reader thinking about the value-related assumptions from which he or she teaches or will teach." This intent has been met, and in a manner that is always provocative, at times amusing, and in places inspiring.

Read on, you're in for a rich experience.

Jack R. Fraenkel

Preface

This is a book written for teachers—prospective and practicing. It is not written for academicians, although we have, of course, been constantly aware of our university colleagues' glances over our shoulders. We see it as appropriate for undergraduate courses—educational foundations, general methods, methods of teaching social studies or English—at the elementary or secondary levels, as well as for graduate courses and in-service programs for practicing teachers and supervisors.

We are concerned with concepts and distinctions that seem suited to value-related teaching decisions and therefore are usable by teachers. We are less concerned with fine intellectual distinctions than some of our university colleagues might wish—not because such distinctions are unimportant, but because we do not view them as functional for the day-to-day realities of classroom life.

It should be noted, too, that our discussion of values is not based solely on writings in the discipline of philosophy. It also owes much to work in political science, to an anthropological view of the role of values, and to research in the psychological aspects of valuing. In short, we are more concerned with values as cultural, political, and psychological phenomena than with the analytic distinctions with which philosophers grapple in searching for intellectual rigor, precision, and consistency.

Even our citing of references may be bothersome to academicians, but we hope that the majority of our readers will find them useful. Our aim was to provide not the "original" sources of ideas, but references to which the interested reader can turn for further discussion. These readings generally will provide original sources for those who wish them.

This book is founded on the authors' faith in rationality. We believe that rationality in valuing is good, and that value-related teaching decisions will be better if made through an open, rational process. This commitment to rationality implies a warning: Be alert throughout to our biases. We have tried to lay out a rationale and its implications, pulling our assumptions into the open, partly as an illustrative exercise that may help you to explicate and scrutinize your own frame of reference. But these are subtle and complex matters. We urge you to subject what we say to continuous examination as you read, and to guard against unwarranted conclusions on our part.

We should also mention that this is *not* a book in methodology, though its narrative sections depict teachers in action. It is intended to engage the reader in thinking about the value-related assumptions from which he or she teaches or will teach. It is full of implications about how to interact with students; but to draw them out and develop them was beyond our present scope. This book is intended to be heuristic in nature. To spell out all the methodological implications not only would have taken too much space, but also would have belied our faith in the ability of teachers to think for themselves.

The theoretical framework of this book is the outcome of several years of graduate work, public school teaching, participation in teacher training, curriculum development, and consultant work by the senior author. He first set out to write the book alone; but after much of the basic manuscript was on paper, he sought a collaborator. Someone was needed who could provide critical feedback and apply a literary flair to the writing of the narrative sections intended to involve the reader in thinking about the substantive content of each chapter. The Shaver-Strong association has, we trust, created a more readable, applicable book. Our frequent discussions have also resulted in introspection and expansion for both of us—and the volume is much more than either of us could have produced alone.

Any endeavor of this sort rests on the contributions of people too numerous to name. However, the early intellectual prodding of Donald W. Oliver, one of the seminal thinkers in American education and a master teacher at Harvard, cannot go without mention and thanks. Jack Fraenkel, editor of the series of which this book is a part, has taken the time to make thoughtful and helpful criticisms of the manuscript. We would like to thank the following reviewers: Lawrence E. Metcalf, University of Illinois; Jack L. Nelson, Rutgers, The State University; and Michael Scriven, University of California, Berkeley. We also found Glen Casto's critique of the material on Piaget and Kohlberg in Chapter 7 very helpful. These contributions, and all those un-named ones from our practicing colleagues in elementary and secondary schools and from our university colleagues, are greatly appreciated. Special thanks are also due Billie Sue McNeil and Karen Casto for typing and other manuscript contributions "above and beyond."

One last note: You will find two kinds of inserts throughout the book. One kind consists of quotations and cartoons that illustrate or elaborate on points being made in the text. These are meant to be read with the text. We hope that they will expand your thinking on the issues being discussed. The second type of boxed material refers you to vignettes and value explorations located at the end of each chapter. We suggest that you first read each chapter through quickly to get a sense of its thrust. Then, on a second reading, turn to the vignettes and value explorations as you come to the boxed references. They should help to illustrate the ideas in the text and assist you to apply them to your own teaching decisions.

Now on to the main body of the book. We only hope that you find your involvement in it nearly as exciting as we have found ours!

James P. Shaver
William Strong

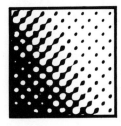

Facing Value Decisions:
Rationale-building for Teachers

Do You Want to Deal with Values?

It has become fashionable in recent years to speak of the school's "hidden curriculum"—school experiences that result in unintended, unplanned, even unsuspected and undesired student learning. The "hidden" curriculum is typically contrasted with the "formal" curriculum—the experiences purposely set up to accomplish the intended, although often not explicitly stated, goals and objectives of the various curriculum areas. The hidden curriculum includes the unintended implications of content and of teaching behavior, as well as the many "noninstructional" encounters that students have with teachers and other school people. Much of the hidden curriculum has to do with values,[1] even in subject areas that are frequently considered "value free"—such as science and mathematics.

Values in the Classroom

Consider, for example, a biology class in which none of the assignments or class discussions has to do with ecological problems. Or how about a chemistry class that does not deal with ways of assessing the deterioration of the environment—for example, by using lab techniques to measure air- or water-pollution levels. The decision not to deal with such matters in a science class may be justifiable, particularly in the context of a particular class as opposed to a total curriculum. But what does such a decision convey to the student about the values of the teacher and the school, and about the kinds of intellectual activities and goals he himself should value?

Even the methods used in teaching science may have important

---

[1] We define a value as a principle or standard of worth. This definition will be developed more fully in Chapter 2.

value implications. For example, students kill and dissect frogs in a biology class: What are they being taught about the value of life? [2]

. . . [B]ills have been proposed before legislatures, over the years, to legalize the use of live animals, including cats and dogs, in high school science experiments. One of the arguments has been that by experimenting on a dog or a cat, the child will assume a more impersonal and objective attitude toward animals. Never mind the fact that we will be teaching our children to repress emotions of empathy and compassion. One high school student was reportedly traumatized during a diabolical experiment conducted by the biology teacher dissecting a half-anesthetized screaming kitten in front of the class. One cannot help but wonder what psychological effect experiences like this will have on the developing child.

— Judith Schmidt. *Family Weekly*, December 23, 1973.

The methods and content of science bring values into the classroom in yet another way. The image of the scientist in his laboratory, working long hours, neglecting his family, and abstaining from the more usual and mundane pleasures of life as he follows his commitment to the search for truth, is part of the lore of Twentieth Century America. As Bronowski (1965, pp. 99–100) has put it:

In practicing science, we accept from the outset an end which is laid down for us. The end of science is to discover what is true about the world. The activity of science is directed to seek the truth, and it is judged by that criterion. *We can practice science only if we value the truth.* (Italics ours.)

What is truth to the scientist? George Gaylord Simpson, a Professor of Vertebrate Paleontology at Harvard University, gave the following answer (1962, p. 11):

The concept of truth in science is . . . quite special. It implies nothing eternal and absolute but only a high degree of confidence after adequate objective self-testing and self-correction.

So science has imbedded in it such values as objectivity and the willingness to change one's beliefs when faced with contradictory evidence.

---

[2] If this question seems worth pursuing, and we believe it is, see George K. Russell's (1972) discussion of "Vivisection and the true aims of biological education." This and all subsequent references may be found in the Bibliography.

To the extent that science teaching is faithful to science, the hidden curriculum should reflect such values; indeed, one may even expect them to be an intentional part of the formal curriculum. On the other hand, science is sometimes taught in a noninquiring, absolute way that belies these commitments—but implies others.

In addition, the scientist's pursuit of truth can have tremendous implications for and impact on the values of society. Can science be taught adequately if these reverberations are ignored? For example, the Copernican view of the universe—that the earth and humankind are *not* at the center of things—shocked a world whose theology was built on the opposite premise. And Galileo's demonstration of the truth of the Copernican theory won him condemnation for heresy. The fantastic destructiveness of nuclear power, unleashed by physical scientists seeking to understand natural phenomena, raised as never before the question: Should scientific research be done without consideration of the morality of its possible applications? Research in biogenetics has raised the same sort of questions.

Research in the social sciences is also likely to have tremendous value implications. Two recent examples come from sensitive areas—race (ethno-cultural differences) and sex. Psychologist Arthur Jensen entered the first of these areas in his research. He wondered (Jensen, 1969) whether the available data did not support the hypothesis of genetic differences in intelligence between blacks and whites. The reactions of blacks and whites indicated how value-laden that "scientific" question was. Jensen's reports were greeted with cries of "racist," and there were attempts to keep him from teaching on the University of California, Berkeley campus and from speaking at professional meetings.[3]

In the area of sex, the example of Alfred Kinsey, zoologist turned sexologist, illustrates how the commitment to search for empirical truth, combined with a particular scientific perspective, can have a controversial impact on personal and societal values. Kinsey's scientific training and early research in zoology were taxonomic in nature—that is, he was concerned with classifying animals into natural, related groups. For example, from his collection of over four million gall wasps, he gathered and analyzed data to determine whether the categories being used by entomologists to classify insects were adequate. When Kinsey was moved to study human sexual behavior, he brought with him the data-gathering approach of his zoological research. He collected enormous quantities of information in interviews with close to twenty thousand men and women. The results, published in two controversial volumes, *Sexual Behavior in the Human Male* (1948) and *Sexual Behavior in the Human Female* (1953), were blockbusters. Among other things, Kinsey said his data indicated that people's sexual behavior often bore little relation to the sexual mores of our society.

[3] Those interested in this still-percolating controversy (stimulated by the entry into the fray of William Shockley, a physicist turned geneticist) will want to check sources such as the following: Jensen (1969, 1973), Rice (1973), Scriven (1970), Winkler (1973).

Although the approach taken by Kinsey and his associates was quantitative, it had important implications for society's values. To many people, Kinsey's findings suggested that society's sexual moral standards were a facade, a sham to cover up what really was going on. To some, the implication seemed clear: Let's not pretend that we disapprove of sexual relations before or outside of marriage when our behavior indicates otherwise. It has been argued that the Kinsey volumes were a major factor in liberalizing—or, as some would put it, loosening—the moral standards of the following decades.

Although Kinsey apparently viewed his works as purely scientific documents, others saw them as "highly tendentious," with "a distinct permissivist bias," projecting a "fundamentally materialistic notion of human sexuality" (Robinson, 1972, p. 100). This latter subject—the implied standards by which personal sexual experiences are to be judged—bothered some people as much as did the implied rejection of long-standing sexual mores.

Robinson (1972, pp. 100, 102), in reviewing two biographies of Kinsey, commented:

> There was some justice in these [criticisms]. Kinsey never recognized that by asking certain questions rather than others he committed himself to a particular conception of sexual life, which while "objective" in the sense that it did not contradict the facts, was nonetheless partial. He tended to ask about physical acts, not about the internal states accompanying them, and he naturally found it easier to measure the quantity rather than the quality of acts (Robinson, 1972, pp. 100, 102).

Science teachers, then, must be aware that science content may have a potent hidden curriculum bearing on the value orientations of their students and the broader society. In addition, they must consider this basic question: Can science instruction be adequate if it does not deal explicitly with the value implications of scientific findings?

What happens when a young, earnest teacher meets a bunch of three- and four-year-old kids for a lesson about drums? See "A Lesson for Anthony," p. 9, for a glimpse of how the hidden curriculum can communicate values in a profound and powerful way.

Similar questions need to be raised in areas other than science, of course. A math teacher scolds a student for not appreciating the beauty of geometry. The students who are counseled into courses that call for the practical application of math concepts, such as business math, all come from working-class backgrounds. What is being implied about the kinds of knowledge to be valued, or the kinds of people who are most valued?

The inevitability of dealing with values in the social studies curriculum may seem clear when teachers seek such goals as "good citizenship." But what about the social studies teacher who sees the job as teaching social science and history concepts that have been adapted and simplified so that the students can understand them? What if this instructor teaches about hypothesis testing and presents content on such topics as poverty, alcoholism and drug use, and mental illness, without raising related issues of social policy? What if he or she teaches a neat, academically sound account of the Civil War, its causes and results—but doesn't comment on the morality of slavery or on the behavior of whites and blacks during the Reconstruction period?

What are the implied value priorities? What value-related outcomes are likely in regard to: The importance of dealing with abstract ideas as compared to the nasty realities of societal controversy? The importance of confronting basic moral issues? And perhaps most important of all, the student's tendency to value the school in terms of its relevance to the world "out there"—especially as this world touches on his own life?

In curriculum areas such as music, art, and literature the central place of values probably is even more immediately obvious. After all, the school's esthetic curriculum is concerned with the student's valuing of beauty, and, in that sense, values are expected to be an explicit part of the formal curriculum. But as one would expect, values enter through the hidden curriculum as well. The tendency of art and music teachers to assume that their sophisticated views of esthetics have intrinsic value will be discussed later. Among literature teachers there is a tendency to assume not only that students should analyze everything they read, but also that some particular style of literary criticism is *the* frame of reference from which every person should approach the reading of fiction. Even more important, attempts to change black dialect and the failure to discuss minority literature often have value implications that every conscientious teacher must confront.

Do these ideas apply to your own area of teaching? Give Value Exploration 1, p. 11, a try.

The Extracurricular Curriculum

The obvious point is that *no* curriculum is value free. Values and value implications are an inevitable part of instruction. But it is also important to remember that as each teacher interacts with students, in and out of the classroom, as part of the social and political system of the school, much "teaching" takes place.

A teacher scolds a tenth-grade boy and girl for walking down the hall with their arms around each other. A principal asks a seventh-grade teacher to send him a list of the boys whose hair has reached an objectionable length, and the teacher does so. An elementary teacher chastises her children for wearing muddy boots into the classroom or for not putting books back on the shelves neatly. In each instance, the teacher is saying something to the students about his or her own values and about what he or she believes the students' values ought to be.

© 1973 United Feature Syndicate, Inc.

There is no use pretending that teachers can avoid such value-related decisions. We must act, and our values will be a major influence in determining how we treat students. The danger again is in pretending that what we do is "value free." Such a pretense allows unexamined assumptions and biases to influence our behavior. And the impacts on our students will often be detrimental to the objectives that we consciously seek.

Frame of Reference

The question, then, is not *whether* you will deal with values or *whether* your values will affect what you do. It is rather, *what* will you do about values, and *will you be aware* of the influence of your own values and make it as conscious and rational as possible? Charles Beard, a historian who examined the secondary school social studies curriculum in the 1930s, emphasized the importance of the latter point (Beard, 1934, p. 182):

> Every human being brought up in society inevitably has in mind a frame of social knowledge, ideas, and ideals—a more or less definite pattern of things deemed *necessary*, things deemed *possible*, and things deemed *desirable*; and to this frame or pattern, his thought and action will be

more or less consciously referred. This frame may be large or small; it may embrace an immense store of knowledge or little knowledge; it may be well organized with respect to categories of social thought or confused and blurred in organization; and the ideal element in it may represent the highest or lowest aspirations of mankind. But frame there is in every human mind.

. . . Since all things known cannot be placed before children in the school room, there must and will be, inevitably, a selection, and the selection will be made with reference to some frame of knowledge and values, more or less consciously established in the mind of the selector.

For purposes of simplicity, we will use the term *frame of reference* to refer to what Beard calls "a frame of social knowledge, ideas, and ideals." In considering values and teaching decisions, it is crucial to underscore Beard's point that a frame of reference is not something that some people have and others don't. *Each* of us has a frame of reference; our values are a very important part of that frame; and *each person's* actions are influenced by his or her frame. A person who is unaware of the impact of his or her frame of reference will unthinkingly apply and impose the elements, including the values, in it.

A big-shouldered shop teacher slams his fist into a shop table and summons Carlos Sanchez into his office. The boy's mouth goes dry with fear. See "Shop Sketch," p. 12, for a check on Carlos's frame of reference as well as your own.

From Frame to Rationale

Many of the elements in one's frame of reference are unexplicated, unexamined assumptions. If your behavior as a teacher is to be as rational as possible, these assumptions need to be brought into the open, stated as clearly as possible, examined for accuracy and consistency, and used as the basis for decisions about your instructional and other behavior toward students (for example, in the lunchroom or during hall duty). The product of this process of explicating and clarifying one's frame of reference we call a *rationale.* Defined more precisely, a rationale is the statement and explication of the basic principles upon which your school behavior (both in the formal classroom setting and during the other encounters within the school's social and political system) is based.

The development of an explicit rationale for teaching, as distinct from a largely implicit frame of reference, is essential but not easy. Among the areas needing clarification are your assumptions about society and the school's relationship to it, about the nature of children and how they learn, about the nature of values. The critical examination of your unconscious and frequently cherished assumptions in these areas is not something that you will accomplish overnight, or even during an undergraduate course or an inservice training program. In fact, you are not likely ever to arrive at a completely explicated and polished rationale.

A rationale, like the person who is attempting to develop it, evolves and is always in the process of becoming. Your rationale may become more explicit, more comprehensive, more logical in the interrelationship of its parts, clearer in its implications for your behavior as a teacher. But it ought never to be considered final, for that would imply that you have stopped changing and growing.

One important reason for developing a rationale is to avoid the unthinking imposition of your beliefs on your students. Equally important from a pragmatic point of view is the need for a systematic, well-grounded basis from which to explain, even defend, your instructional behavior to administrators and parents. In English and social studies, for example, teachers challenged for raising controversial issues in their classrooms have gotten into trouble because their justification was not much deeper than "Controversy is good." Certainly, in a democratic society a more profound and persuasive justification can be developed.

When schooling touches on values, parents are particularly likely to react emotionally. For that reason, any teacher who decides to deal with values explicitly (recognizing, of course, that no teacher can avoid dealing with values implicitly) ought to have a conscious rationale as a foundation for his or her approach. Communication of this rationale to other teachers, to the principal, and even to the superintendent, may help to insure that vital support will be available if needed. Moreover, going through the process of discussing your rationale with other school people may help you to communicate it later to parents and to persuade them of its soundness.

Our Intent

The school's role vis-à-vis values often comes up in conversations, perhaps more among lay people than among educators, and in such places as the newspaper columns written by Max Rafferty. Frequently the statements made there reflect one of the following polar positions:

Teachers have no business dealing with values. The school's role is to teach skills—in reading, writing, and arithmetic, and in vocational areas. The values of youth are the business of home and church.

The school is an instrument of society. Teachers must, therefore, be deeply involved in shaping the values of young people—from instilling important personal values, such as honesty, to inculcating values of fundamental importance, such as patriotism. If they do otherwise, teachers are derelict in their duty.

Whether your own view is reflected in one of the above statements or not, we hope to get you to examine your position on this critical matter. Our intent is to have an impact on your frame of reference. In particular, we hope to make you more aware of your value-related decisions as a teacher, to engage you in building a rationale for dealing with values, and to provide you with some ideas that will help you to develop an explicit basis for handling values. Of the many matters that are central to the task of constructing such a rationale, none is more basic than reflection on the nature of values. And we turn to that next.

A Lesson for Anthony[4]

Problem *As you read the following play, identify the "hidden" curriculum.*

Scene: A day nursery. Crowded into the room are children, teachers, play equipment, books, a set of drums. As the lights come up, the three- and four-year-old children are gathered around the teacher-for-the-day and the drums. The children are noisy and talkative, obviously excited about this special event. Their pudgy fingers reach out to touch the shiny enameled finish of the drums, the taut skins, and the crisp circles of brass. The teacher's name is Mr. Barker. He is a young man with an earnest face. He is nervous, but he smiles in a teacherly way as he stands up, rubbing the edges of his mouth. They have been talking about the names of the drums.

Mr. Barker: Hey, that's pretty good, you guys. We got all the names now. Bass, snare, cymbals, right? Not bad, not bad! Now the bass, you see, it's carried up front—like in a parade. And the snare—well, you see those in the dance bands, right? Every dance band has snares to give the *rhythm.* Can you say that word? *Rhythm. (Mr. Barker pauses to frown at some troublemakers at the edge of the circle; the children seem to be getting restless.)*

Mike: Hey, I wanna hit it! *(He reaches for one of the drumsticks.)*

Mr. Barker: Whoa there, young man. Just a minute now. Can you say *rhythm?*

---

[4] Many of the vignettes in this book are adapted from material field-tested with prospective teachers (Strong, 1973).

Mike: Uhhhh. *(He looks puzzled.)* Riv-vum.

Mr. Barker: No, no. The word is RHYTHM.

Trudy: Ribbon, ribbon! *(She is making faces at another girl.)*

Mike: Uhhh, riv-vum; riv-vum.

Mr. Barker: Ri-thum.

Mike: Ri——Uhmmm.

Mr. Barker: Nope, not quite. You almost have it. *Ri-thum.* That's what the snares do in the dance band. They make the rhythm. One, two, three, four—one, two, three . . . *(He begins to clap his hands, and the students quickly catch the beat; they clap along for about ten seconds.)* Okay, okay. That's enough, gang. Hold it down. *(Most youngsters are still clapping.)* Hey, now—I think that's about *enough.* QUIET! *(The noise drops off.)* Okay, that's a little *better.* Now we're gonna have a *march,* so who wants to be the leader?

Anthony: Me, me! *(He is waving his hand.)*

Mr. Barker: Hey, all right, Anthony. You're it. You're the leader. You get out in the middle there; and everybody line up, right? Right behind Anthony! *(The teacher's smile seems tighter, more restrained.)*

Anthony: I gonna be a leader. *(He scrambles up and races to the middle of the room; all of the children crowd around him in a confused knot of jabbering and noise. They are excited.)*

Mike: Hey, I hit the drum now? *(He is pulling at Mr. Barker's shirt.)*

Mr. Barker: Quiet, now. QUIET. Mike, you get out there for the march. C'mon now, hurry-up—and don't *hang.* *(The frown is back.)* Now, I said line up, didn't I? So LINE UP! Let's go now! Carol, get in line. *(The confusion continues for about thirty seconds, but finally some semblance of a line begins to form behind Anthony as well as around him. Everybody is talking.)* QUIET, now. SETTLE DOWN!

Jerry: I gonna march, march, march— *(He is out of line.)*

Debbie: We start now? Start it, Anthony.

Mr. Barker: Quiet down, you kids. You'll have to be quiet or we don't have the march. Marsha, Pam—you two get back in line and hush up. *(He has moved out toward the middle of the room, hunching his shoulders together aggressively.)*

Victor: One, two, three, four. . . .

Mike: Can I hit the drum? Teacher? Can. . . .

Mr. Barker: Okay. Now Anthony, you know which foot is your *left?*

Anthony: Uh-huh. *(He lifts his left foot and stands teetering on his right. A big grin creases his freckled face. He is obviously proud that he knows his left foot from his right.)*

Mr. Barker: Beautiful, Anthony. *Real* good. Now I want everybody to do just like Anthony here, right? Left foot up. Got that? *Left* foot. *(The children watch Anthony and switch from left to right to left. It is hard because some of them are facing the other way. The room resembles a training ground for unsteady young storks.)*

Debbie: We gonna start?

Mr. Barker: Real good. Hold up that left foot now, 'cause when we march we always start with the left foot first. Got that? *(Children are starting to topple back and forth, and Mr. Barker frowns again.)* Left foot, not your right. This is real important so we can all keep in step with the drum. Got that, Anthony?

Anthony: Uh-huh. *(Still standing on his right foot, his left in the air, Anthony blinks affirmatively. He is concentrating. His tongue curls over his front lip.)*

Jeff: My leg hurts. *(He has put his left foot down.)*

Judy: March, march, march—

Mr. Barker: Okay, everybody; let's get ready! *(He rushes back to the bass drum and squares himself for the swing; then he begins pounding the drum with big booming strokes.)* Go, Anthony!

Anthony: MARCH! *(Anthony begins HOPPING on his right leg across the tile floor in time to the bass drum. His tongue is still between his teeth. Several kids start hopping after him. Others look puzzled. Finally they all start hopping.)*

Mr. Barker: (The drum stops pounding, and Mr. Barker moves out toward Anthony, arms flailing a criss-crossing motion in front of him as his head wags an angry "no.") NO! NO! NO! ANTHONY! *(His face is fierce.)* I SAID *MARCH!* A hush falls over the room at this outburst, and Anthony walks to the furthest corner, away from the drums. He sits down on the floor near the coat racks and pulls his knees up, putting his head down in a kind of fetal gathering in of himself. Mr. Barker is shaking his head. He and the other adults in the room cannot coax Anthony to get up and participate in the new march. The others finally give up and go back to the drums, where the children are gathered. Mr. Barker lines up the children again. This time Victor is the leader. The children begin marching as the lights go down slowly, a single spot lingering at Anthony's feet. The children's bodies become shadows. A bass drum thumps softly in the background, fading into silence as the light goes out.

Follow-up *This is a true story, with names changed to protect the guilty. What assumptions about kids and schooling does Mr. Barker seem to be making?*

What are the youngsters learning about music class? About music? About teachers? About school?

One of the readers of this manuscript commented, "I wonder if we shouldn't ask what Shaver and Strong's values are, in putting this poor guy Barker in the pillory." We think that's an excellent suggestion. Each of the narratives on the following pages should be examined for our hidden value assumptions.

Value Exploration 1

Take a single concept or skill from a subject you know something about and see if you can ferret out its value implications.

For example, if you're planning to teach reading at one of the elementary levels, you might ask yourself what values are implied in a basal reading program (one that utilizes a strictly controlled vocabulary) versus a language-experience approach (one that utilizes the range of vocabulary already possessed by the student). Also in the area of reading, you might consider what values are subtly communicated in books where minorities are shown mostly in blue-collar roles and women are shown doing menial household chores.

On a more general level, you might try to frame an articulate response to Neil Postman's (1970) contentions in "The Politics of Reading": (1) that print is no longer the dominant form of communication in this country; (2) that new patterns of mass media communication disrupt old patterns of thought and social organization; and (3) that it is reactionary to argue that other media cannot take the place of print. Postman is asking a question that you must answer with something more than clichés and platitudes: Why teach reading? What values would be implied if we decided not to teach reading?

By the same token, if you're planning to teach a subject at the secondary level, you might examine one of its fundamental concepts in terms of implicit and explicit value assumptions. In English, for example, you might consider the concept of "good" English. What is it? How does it differ from "bad" English? Can "good" English be used by "bad" people (or vice versa)? Since language is linked to self-concept, how can the valuing of oneself be affected when teachers give speech and writing patterns value-laden labels? Do public schools have any *right* to attempt to change the dialects of minority students? And so on.

In a subject like mathematics, you might consider the value implications of concepts such as "simplicity" and "elegance" within a formula or proof. Why do mathematicians value the "simplicity" of the Pythagorean theorem or of Einstein's famous statement $E = mc^2$? And should the solution of an equation by pure rational means (rather than by the "brute force" method of plugging in numbers on a trial-and-error basis) be judged to be better *esthetically*? Is it even possible for most youngsters to comprehend the "beauty" in mathematics—a beauty based on conciseness, lack of ambiguity, and internal logic? What experiences might promote an appreciation of that beauty in the elementary and secondary grades? What experiences might work against gaining these values? Should math teachers cultivate such an appreciation?

Shop Sketch

Problem *What do Carlos's reactions tell you about his frame of reference? How about the teacher's frame of reference and implicit assumptions about teaching?*

Outside, the sky is clearing off.

Lon O'Hara, shop teacher and assistant football coach, grins to himself as he thinks about the crunch of pads and flesh tonight under the Friday night fieldlights. He slams his sledgelike fist into one of the oak drawing tables as he makes his way toward the drill press where two boys are working.

He is six feet, two inches tall—220 pounds of wedge-shaped muscle. His shoulders are thick knots beneath his white shop coat. He has red, curly hair and a red beard that needs trimming; his eyes burn like blue ice. On weekends, he climbs mountains, skydives, charges the surf, and drinks beer by the pitcher. Living, he sometimes says, is simply a matter of taking life by the throat.

The boys look up, eyes white behind their goggles.

"Carlos," he says. "You come with me."

The boy swallows and looks at his friend. Lon O'Hara is striding toward his office, shoulders bunched beneath the coat. The boy peels off his goggles and hurries to catch up. The door squishes closed behind them. The teacher's face is thoughtful, silent.

"Yes sir?"

Lon O'Hara stares at him.

The buzz and snap of the arc welder are barely audible.

"How old are you, Sanchez?"

"Fifteen."

"This is your first year here, I take it."

The boy blinks and nods.

"I thought so. Well, Carlos, I'm going to put this to you straight. You have the distinction of having made the O'Hara list." He opens his gradebook to a marked section and stares at it. "This is where I keep the list, Carlos."

The boy eyes the gradebook for a moment, working his mouth into a dry question. "Uh, what kind of list? I ain't done nothin'." His hands are jammed into his jeans.

"You're wrong there, Carlos. Everybody who makes the O'Hara list has done *something*." O'Hara flexes his shoulders, and the coat seams strain. "I know everything going on out there."

A crash echoes in from the shop, and Carlos begins picking at his front teeth. His eyes are black, narrowing as they focus on his tennis shoes.

"You see, you've been doing a damn good job out there, Carlos. I like your work—I mean, what I've seen so far. You've got real potential."

Carlos lifts his eyebrows; his weight shifts.

"Not just anybody gets on my list, Carlos."

O'Hara stretches across his desk and pulls a tattered paperback book from a large stack. He thumbs the cover.

"This book, Carlos—well, it's one I thought you might be sort of interested in. Metal sculpture, you know?" He begins flipping pages. "You interested in that sort of thing?"

The boy shrugs as a small grin forms at the corners of his mouth.

"I just thought you might be," O'Hara says. "I noticed those drawings on your notebook." He pauses to wink. "Maybe you'd like to take it home over the weekend."

Follow-up *Think about Carlos's original reaction to his "summons" from Mr. O'Hara. What values does he assume are guiding the teacher's behavior?*

What curriculum values does Mr. O'Hara express as he hands Carlos the book on metal sculpture?

Get together with some friends and talk about situations where a teacher's implicit values affected your behavior, either positively or negatively.

Values—What Are They?

Perhaps we have put it off too long already, but if our deliberations are to be productive, we must define the term *value*. There are many theories of valuation, and value is defined in many different ways.[1] There is no sense pretending that any one definition is the right one. But several years of curriculum work (Oliver & Shaver, 1966; Shaver & Berlak, 1968; Shaver & Larkins, 1969, 1973) suggest that the following definition is a useful one: *Values* are our standards and principles for judging worth. They are the criteria by which we judge "things" (people, objects, ideas, actions, and situations) to be good, worthwhile, desirable; or, on the other hand, bad, worthless, despicable; or, of course, somewhere in between these extremes. We may apply our values consciously. Or they may function unconsciously, as part of the influence of our frames of reference, without our being aware of the standards implied by our decisions.

Some Distinctions

It is important to distinguish between *values* and *value judgments*. The latter are assertions we make based on our values. A teacher who says, "Duke, you should get to class on time," is making a value judgment. What is the value (the criterion) that leads to that judgment? It may be *punctuality*. It may be *classroom order* (a student coming in tardy disrupts the class). It may be *respect* (coming in tardy implies a lack of respect for the teacher or the school) or, at a somewhat different level, *self-worth* (the tardy student is a threat to the teacher's conception of her own self-worth).

[1] For a comprehensive bibliography on the theory of value, see Rescher (1969, pp. 149–186).

Statements that appear to be directives or factual claims often are implicit value judgments. For example, a teacher directive as simple as "Open your textbooks" contains implicit value judgments such as "Everyone in class should be doing the same thing."

Value judgments typically do not state the values being applied. In order to determine whether our assertions and/or behavior are rationally related to our values, it is important to distinguish the value judgment from the underlying value or values. Such self-criticism may move us to modify a value to be consistent with what we are saying and/or doing; or, on the other hand, we may modify our assertions or our behavior to make them consistent with a value. Value judgments are based on values that can, and should, be explicated in the interests of clarity and consistency.

Do the distinctions between factual claims or directives, value judgments, and values make sense to you? Value Exploration 2, p. 31, provides the opportunity to put these distinctions to work and run a self-check on your understanding.

Values—Affective or Cognitive?

In answering the question: What are values? it is also important to distinguish between affective objectives—those emphasizing feelings and emotion (Krathwohl, Bloom, & Masia, 1964, p. 7)—and cognitive objectives —those dealing with knowledge and with intellectual abilities and skills (Bloom, 1956, p. 7). Whether you see values as one or the other, or as a combination of both, can have serious implications for your teaching.

With the publication of the *Taxonomy of Educational Objectives: Cognitive Domain* (Bloom, 1956), educationists began to make a fetish of a new activity—analyzing objectives to determine whether they fall into the cognitive or affective domain. Such analysis and categorization can be interesting as an intellectual exercise, and helpful as a means of clarifying what one wants to teach, how to teach it, and how to test to determine if one has taught it. In the area of values, however, the emphasis on categorizing objectives as cognitive or affective has not always had positive results. It has led some to think in terms of a dichotomy—an objective is *either* cognitive *or* affective, not both. For some reason, many educators see values as falling exclusively into the affective domain—that is, as involving only feelings and emotion. The result has been that many teachers have been encouraged to throw up their hands in despair (or perhaps, in some cases, relief!) and say, "Oh, values are only feelings. Therefore, we can't deal with them in the classroom." (This conclusion, of course, ignores the fact that they will be doing so anyway, consciously or not.) For some, values as affective objectives take on a mystic aura—they are private inner feelings with which one hesitates to interfere.

It is critical, then, to recognize that although values do embody and convey feeling, values as we have defined them are much more than emotions. Values and valuing clearly fall into the cognitive domain because standards are concepts, and valuing involves intellectual abilities and skills (Bloom, 1956, p. 7). Values have intellectual meaning that can be defined and clarified. And values can be compared, related to one another, and consciously applied as criteria.

For example, honesty is a value by which we frequently judge the actions of ourselves and others. The term "honesty" does evoke feelings. For most people, "honest" behavior calls forth a positive emotive reaction, and we have negative feelings toward people or actions that we consider "dishonest." But each of us, although we may not have taken the time and effort to define it precisely, also has a *concept* of honesty. Without too much additional thought, you could undoubtedly describe right now what you mean by "honest"—for example, what kinds of behavior you would consider to be honest or dishonest.

So values are both cognitive and affective—an important point to keep in mind. Whether or not you view values in this way is critical, because it will influence how *you* deal with values as a teacher. Will you shuffle aside proposals to treat values specifically in the classroom, on the excuse that values are nonintellectual and therefore not fit subjects for instruction in cognitively oriented curriculum areas? If you do deal with values, will you be concerned with more than emotion and feeling? Will you also deal with values as concepts and with valuing as an intellectual process that can be rigorous?

Values—What They Aren't

It is common to hear educators use the terms *values* and *attitudes* interchangeably, as if they were synonymous. Often discussion will reveal that the person has not stopped to consider in what ways *value* and *attitude* might refer to different concepts. Just as instructional decision making can be more precise if values are distinguished from value judgments, so our thinking can be sharpened by distinguishing values from attitudes.

An *attitude,* as commonly defined by psychologists, is a number of interrelated beliefs and feelings focused on some object. The "object" may be a group of actions (e.g., the U.S. involvement in the Vietnam War), people (such as blacks or whites), situations (presidential elections), or things (Ford automobiles). Or it may be an individual action, person, situation, or thing. We have attitudes *toward*—for example, toward long hair or a particular student who has long hair, or toward black Americans or a particular student who is black. Our attitudes encompass and are affected by a number of factors, including our factual beliefs and our values.[2] Each of us has thousands of attitudes. The number is limited only by our range of experience and the number of objects about which we have feelings and beliefs.

Values, on the other hand, as standards of worth, are a more fundamental aspect of our frames of reference. They underlie our attitudes and are fewer in number. One psychologist (Rokeach, 1971, 1973) who has worked extensively with attitudes and values estimates that while each of us has thousands of attitudes, we are likely to have only several dozen values.

In one sense, then, attitudes and value judgments are similar in that both are based consciously or unconsciously on one's values as well as on factual assumptions. In deciding what you, as a teacher, should do in regard to values, it is important to be clear in your mind whether you are concerned with value judgments, attitudes, or the underlying value and factual beliefs. For instance, do you simply want the student to conform to your value judgments about classroom behavior, or do you want him to understand (and perhaps share) the values that underlie those judgments? Or, to ask a more poignant question, do *you* know what values underlie your value judgment that "Johnny should be quiet!"? Are you interested in changing your students' attitudes toward black Americans or classical music, or in helping them to clarify their own values and strive for consistency between value and attitude?

Which type of objective you seek will have serious implications for your behavior as a teacher. But equally important, different types of objectives call for different justifications. For example, you may find yourself in rough territory when you try to convince parents that you should be shaping their children's attitudes toward minority groups. But it may be less difficult to persuade parents that your role should include helping students to clarify their values and use them as conscious criteria against which to match attitudes and value judgments.

In the opening chapter of *Hard Times,* Charles Dickens presents Mr. Thomas Gradgrind, owner of a British private school. Here, in Gradgrind's own words, is the essence of his pedagogical value system:

> Teach these boys and girls nothing but Facts. Facts alone are wanted in life. Plant nothing else, and root out everything else. You can only form minds of reasoning animals upon Facts: nothing else will ever be of any service to them. This is the

[2] *Factual beliefs* are beliefs about what the world *is* like, *has been* like, *can be* like, or *will be* like.

principle on which I bring up my own children, and this is the
principle on which I bring up these children. Stick to the Facts,
Sir!

Should we "stick to the facts"? What happens when a teacher decides that
"planting facts" is *not* the primary goal of education? See "The Experiment," p. 31, for a glimpse of both the cognitive and affective aspects of
values in action.

Three Types of Values

Any decision about what you as a teacher should do about values
must take into account different types of values with which you may be
dealing. Values can be viewed from many different perspectives. Some
people, for example, find it helpful to think of values as being political,
economic, religious, or social in orientation. Categorizing values in that way
is meaningful for social scientists' studies of value systems. But these
categories seem less relevant to the analysis of value-related decisions for
the formal or the hidden curriculum.

A more productive set of categories, one more relevant to commonly
stated school objectives and to the kinds of situations in which teachers
commonly find themselves with students, classifies values as esthetic,
instrumental, and moral. The distinctions between these classifications are
not always clear-cut, but some brief definitions will help outline the meaning
of each and provide valuable background for our consideration of values and
the teacher.

Esthetic Values

Esthetic values are those standards by which we judge beauty—in
art, in music, in literature, as well as in personal appearance, nature, and
even in cookery (the culinary art). Some parts of the school curriculum are
directly concerned with esthetics. Setting teaching goals and making day-to-
day instructional decisions in music, art, and literature demand a direct
consideration of esthetic values.

The connoisseur or specialist in an esthetic field such as art often
develops a complex and subtle system of standards for judging beauty. But
each of us constantly makes esthetic judgments. Moreover, each of us also
tends to allow his or her esthetic values (in regard, for example, to classical
music or to hair style) to take on serious, moralistic tones. Not only is it

frequently difficult for those of us who like the symphony to understand how "those kids" can like rock (and vice versa), but we tend to feel that there is something morally wrong with those who do not share our esthetic values. And the more divergent the esthetic values, the stronger the feeling of moral alienation is likely to be. For example, slight variations in hair styles don't bother most people; but when a male goes so far as to let his hair grow down to his shoulders, and then adds a beard (perhaps unkempt to boot!) and grubby clothes—well!! It's hard for some people to believe that such a man can have decent moral standards. They may even consider him a threat to the whole moral structure of a democratic society!

© 1974 United Feature Syndicate, Inc.

For those who teach esthetic curricula, such as music and art, it is important to remember that the position of esthete too easily degenerates into snobbery. But prejudice based on unthinking esthetic reactions is common to all of us. What should determine the type of music sung in glee club or played in orchestra? Why is it that school people frequently object to students' hair and dress? In short, esthetic values may be the focus of the formal curriculum or they may exert subtle and important influences as part of the hidden curriculum to which we expose students.

Esthetic values even affect classroom routine, as Patty (in the Peanuts cartoon) seems to understand clearly. A conversation at a PTA meeting, "Esthetic Values over Tea and Crumpets," p. 35, raises questions about esthetics and grading of the type you are likely to face as a teacher.

Instrumental Values

As teachers our major and most obvious professional concern is with education—typically with helping our students to learn, moving them from where they are to where we would like them to be. (Note that we did not say, where *they* would like to be. This important distinction reflects an element common to many educators' frames of reference that is too infrequently recognized and challenged.) Courses in education, supervisors, visiting speakers and consultants, and professional journals constantly remind us that to achieve our goals as teachers, we should set objectives and then select appropriate materials and procedures to achieve them. Our success and that of our students are judged by the extent to which the latter do fulfill the stated objectives. In this predominant view of education, the curriculum and our teaching methods are not to be considered good in and of themselves, but are to be judged in terms of their effectiveness as instruments in reaching a desired goal.

Many of our values serve the same function. They are standards set in order to achieve other standards. A principal may object to long hair on male students or casual dress on the part of either males or females on the basis that it is offensive to his own tastes (an esthetic judgment). He is, however, more likely to argue that allowing students to dress and wear their hair in extreme fashions will interfere with the learning atmosphere of the school and be detrimental to the education of all students. Based on that instrumental line of argument, he (or the school board) sets standards for judging hair and clothing styles. Or a teacher insists on a quiet classroom on the assumption that this standard will enhance learning. Values such as these we call *instrumental* values. Instrumental values are not meant to be important in and of themselves, but because they help to attain other ends. They are means to ends.

It is not always easy to decide whether a value is an instrumental one. In fact, one serious problem for teachers is that instrumental values, like esthetic values, often become important in and of themselves. Sometimes they take on moral overtones. Just as teachers may be shocked or affronted by students who do not share their tastes in art, music, or personal dress, so they may consider students "bad," for example, if they talk without permission in the classroom—not stopping to ask themselves whether the talking actually obstructed reaching the end (learning) for which the no-talking rule was established in the first place.

It is important to raise questions not only about the end values we seek in the classroom (e.g., Is knowledge for its own sake good?), but also about the appropriateness of the intermediate instrumental values we set up. You should constantly ask yourself whether you are overlooking the purpose of the instrumental values you have established for your interactions with students in and out of the classroom. Have you unthinkingly allowed these values to become ends in themselves? Or are you maintaining them as tools to be judged by how well they help you to achieve your teaching goals?

It is helpful also to distinguish between *values* and *valued objects*. The latter are also used instrumentally. For example, teachers may use grades to motivate students to work harder, and parents may use automobile privileges to pressure a youngster to do something they deem desirable, such as getting good grades. When an object is used instrumentally, it is often productive to ask what values underlie its use, and then to examine these values. Thus the values that lead teachers and parents to use grades and automobiles as they do may include achievement, working to capacity, optimization of educational opportunity, optimization of job opportunities. And the values that lead students to try for good grades, and thus make grades effective instrumentally, might include status (though this is sometimes negatively related to grades), respect from others, and self-respect. The values that make the lure of an automobile effective instrumentally could include status, mobility, and freedom (e.g., to date whenever one wants).

"Look at my plants there," Mrs. Ashcroft said. "Without the care I provide for them, they simply wouldn't survive. It's the same for youngsters."

Are students like potted plants—dependent for growth on the ministrations of teacher-gardeners? How much order should a teacher impose on students? See "Instrumental Values, Kids, and Potted Plants," p. 37.

Moral Values

As the preceding discussion has implied, we tend to let our esthetic and instrumental values take on moral overtones. This brings us to the third category of values—*moral* values.[3] Moral values are the standards, the principles, by which we judge whether aims or actions are proper. These decisions—about proper aims and actions—we call ethical decisions.

A husband argues that he shouldn't be pressured into going to a bridge party because he prefers to spend the evening alone. You might evaluate a person's behavior on finding a lost purse according to the

---

[3] Some of the prepublication readers of this manuscript were bothered by our distinction between instrumental and moral values. They argued that we should classify values more traditionally as "intrinsic" or "instrumental"—as important in and of themselves or important for what they will accomplish. That classification makes sense in treating valued things (see, e.g., Frankena, 1963, p. 65), but we don't find it very helpful in dealing with teaching decisions. Rokeach (1973, pp. 7–8) uses the terms "instrumental value" and "terminal values," the first alluding to "beliefs concerning desirable modes of conduct" and the second to "desirable end-states of existence." Although we like Rokeach's terminology, his definitions tend to confuse what we consider to be an important distinction between *values* (principles or standards of worth) and *value judgments* based on the values (and on facts as well, of course). We also want to encourage you to think in terms of values that have to do with beauty, standards that are set up to achieve other values, and values that are ends in themselves, and to help you be aware of the tendency to make moral judgments based on the first two types of values. We believe that the esthetic, instrumental, and moral categorization of values is helpful in getting at significant aspects of values and teaching, and hope that the discussions in the following chapters will lead you to agree with us.

"honesty" of his response. Someone opposes capital punishment in the name of the sanctity of human life. In each case, an ethical decision is being made. (Although the decision about whether to go to a bridge party lacks the significant impact on the lives of others that is typically attached to ethical matters, it does involve a matter of interpersonal relations that can take on a serious tone for those involved.) And in each case, a moral value—solitude, honesty, right to life—is used to judge behavior or policy.

Levels of Moral Values These three examples illustrate an important point about moral values: They vary widely in their importance and applicability.

The least significant moral values are *personal preferences*. Expression of such values may well be preceded by such phrases as "I just prefer . . ." We seldom believe that we should impose these values on other people or use them generally to judge others' behavior. But we consider them to be moral values because people do use them *to justify their own behavior* toward others.

Solitude is such a value. The desire for solitude rather than an evening of group activity is largely a matter of individual preference. That value may influence decisions about how to order one's own life. And it is likely to take on considerable significance when it conflicts with someone else's desires—such as those of a wife who wishes to play bridge. No one is likely to deny a person's right to solitude—even the wife who is irritated when her husband insists on it some particular night. But on the other hand, no one—not even the recalcitrant bridge player—is likely to argue that the right to solitude is basic to human existence, applicable to all men as a universal value.[4]

Just the opposite is true of a value such as the sanctity of human life. When a society rejects that value, human existence loses much of its meaning. Whenever life is taken capriciously and without anguish—when Jews are herded to concentration camps for mass slaughter or black Americans are lynched for real or imagined intrusions into white sanctuaries, or innocent Vietnamese civilians are napalmed in their villages—the existence of the perpetrators themselves as well as of those whose lives are threatened become less human and more debased—bestial—in nature. Values like this, deemed essential to human life, are often called *basic* values. In a democratic society, our basic values include commitments to such ideals as equal protection of the law, equal opportunity, freedom of speech, and religious freedom.

Between the extremes of personal preferences, such as solitude— and basic values, such as the sanctity of life—there is a wide range of values

---

[4] Note that we are talking about "solitude" (being alone), not "the right to privacy" (freedom from unwarranted invasion of one's personal life by government officials or other persons).

differing in importance and in breadth of applicability. These we call *middle-level values*. Honesty, for example, is usually considered more than a matter of personal preference. It is sufficiently important that laws are made to punish some kinds of dishonesty.[5] Yet honesty is not usually considered in defining the essential qualities of human existence. Having dishonest people in a society does not make a meaningful human existence impossible. On the contrary, some people even insist that coping with "evil" is a necessary part of *human* existence.

Just as values differ in importance, so some values are not considered applicable to everyone. For example, a member of a religious faith might judge his fellow church members by how regularly they attend church but not apply that value to his other acquaintances. Other middle-level values include such ideals as patriotism, initiative, hard work, cooperation.

Clearly, it doesn't make sense to talk about levels of moral values as if these values could be neatly placed in nicely demarcated categories. Rather, moral values fall along a continuum (see Figure 1), with personal preferences on one end, basic values on the other, and a wide range of middle-level values in between. The boundaries of the three categories are vaguely defined; they overlap, and they are subject to change.

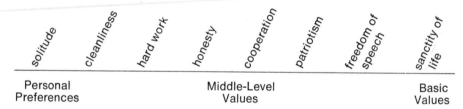

| Personal Preferences | Middle-Level Values | Basic Values |

Figure 1   Levels of Moral Values—A Continuum

It is often hard to decide whether a particular value is a personal preference or a middle-level value, a middle-level or a basic value. Moreover, values may change their place on the continuum over time. Nowadays many people consider education to be a basic right of every citizen in a democracy, a value that would have quite astounded our colonial forefathers. And at any one time, people will differ over where values should be placed on the continuum, as reactions to the hippie generation have made clear. To some people, cleanliness is a matter of personal preference. To others it is clearly at least a middle-level value, and it may even be treated as a basic value during moments of unreflective emotional reaction ("They're like beasts, living in filth like that!").

The point is that moral values do differ in importance and in breadth of applicability. This conclusion is important not as an axiological abstraction, but because it is relevant to the teacher's dealings with values. It is

---

[5] However, it might be more fruitful to think of such laws as protecting the security of potential victims than to see them as imposing honesty on would-be offenders.

vital, as you contemplate what to do about values, that you be clear as to what types of values—esthetic, instrumental, or moral—you are concerned with, and in the case of moral values, that you distinguish the various levels as well.

The time: 4:10 P.M. The place: A high school classroom. What happens when a first-year teacher subtly communicates to youngsters that it's "okay" to come in and talk? See "Moral Values and the 'Teacher-Counselor,' " p. 38.

Interrelationships

It is important to remember that, just as the levels of moral values cannot be thought of as distinct categories, so values cannot always be neatly pigeonholed as esthetic, instrumental, or moral. One reason is that, as we have already noted, esthetic and instrumental values tend to take on moral overtones. One reason for categorizing values is that it forces us to ask whether we are unwittingly making moral judgments based on esthetic or instrumental values.

There is another relationship between esthetic and moral values that needs to be clarified. Esthetic values are a matter of personal taste. Like other values they can be explicated, examined, clarified. But ultimately they are personal because beauty depends upon the individual's internal reaction. No external source, no matter how complex or sophisticated its judgmental scheme, is a more valid judge than you are of what is beautiful to you.[6]

On the other hand, *because moral values are used to justify and judge ethical decisions, and these have impact on other people, moral standards are not merely matters of personal taste.* They also concern those affected, and are legitimately subject to scrutiny and inquiry by them. We

---

[6] That this point of view is not very popular among esthetes goes without saying. Arguing against such a position, Harry Broudy (1973, p. 103) wrote:

> The problem of standards in arts, as far as education is concerned, is solved in the same way as it is solved in other fields of instruction. For the induction of the young, the judgment of the experts, the connoisseurs . . . is the only viable criterion. Authenticity of standards consists not in their originality or uniqueness. They are not authentic *simply* because they are mine but, rather, because I accept and introject them via the same sort of perception, analysis, and reflection as is used by the experts.

Broudy bases his claim for expert over personal standards in art on what we believe to be a fallacious leap from the intellectual discipline of science and scientific standards of truth to the "critical tradition in the arts" and standards for beauty (pp. 95–103). Broudy's frequent references to persons "cultivated" in the arts is reminiscent of the tendency, in years past, to consider people who liked classical art forms as being "cultured." His biases against "popular art" are particularly evident in a section (pp. 110–114) headed, "Serious and Popular Art." (Our query: Can't popular art be serious?)

will argue in Chapters 3 and 6 that, especially in making decisions about public policy, people expect one another to apply the basic values of our democratic society, even though the making of a decision must be a personal matter.

This line of reasoning applies, of course, to personal preferences. They may appear to be similar to esthetic values because they reflect personal predilections. However, personal preferences are used to justify one's behavior toward others and esthetic values are not, and this is a crucial difference. If your standards of beauty do affect your behavior toward other persons, then they fall in the moral field. For example, taste in clothes is an esthetic matter (although, of course, clothing choices have other overtones, such as pleasing one's spouse, conforming to an employer's standards, and being accepted by one's peers). But if you not only prefer certain clothing styles, but also prefer to avoid people who dress differently, you have moved from the field of esthetics to that of ethics. This preference will have an impact on your relationships with other people. And it is important that you treat this preference not as an esthetic one, a matter of personal taste, but as a moral one, in order to make explicit the ethical question: Should this value determine what I do?

There also are important interrelationships between instrumental and moral values. The tendency for instrumental values to take on moral overtones has already been noted. One must also keep in mind that what appear to be moral values may be instrumental. The husband says he prefers solitude to a bridge game. For him, solitude may be not the end, but a means to another end. For example, he may be thinking, "I've got a tough day at the office tomorrow [and efficiency there is a higher level value]. I'll be more on the ball for my work tomorrow if I spend this evening alone."

On the level of basic values, the same reasoning occurs. Not only do instrumental values, such as due process of law, take on importance as ends in and of themselves, but moral values are used instrumentally. A person may promote a housing law in the name of equality of opportunity, all the while thinking that supporting that value is important because it enhances another, higher value—human dignity.

Value Conflict

One further point about the nature of our values. Europeans frequently note that, on the whole, Americans are not only moralists but rationalists as well.[7] That is, we try to justify our actions in terms of moral values at the highest possible level, and we are bothered if our decisions show signs of irrationality.

Americans see inconsistency as a sign of irrationality, and intellec-

---

[7] See, for example, Swedish sociologist Gunnar Myrdal (1944, pp. xlvi–xlvii).

tual consistency—at least surface, public consistency—is valued by our culture. Politicians are criticized for shifting positions; parents worry if they change their minds in coping with their children from one situation to the next; teachers are jarred when they are accused of treating students differently.

It is ironic, in the light of this commitment to consistency, that our value systems are inherently inconsistent. Solitude may be important to a man when a bridge party is involved . . . but what if a buddy calls to invite him to a poker party? Honesty is important . . . but what if a man's girlfriend or wife asks if he likes her new dress—and he doesn't! In each case, countervailing values are likely to prevail. The sanctity of human life is basic . . . but how about people who support capital punishment? Have they no basic values on their side? How about the security of the community or even the right to exact retribution? We rarely recognize our value conflicts, but it is critical to do so if our decisions about how to treat values in the hidden and formal curricula are to be realistic.

One way in which our value systems lack consistency is that, over time, the relative importance of values shifts. A few years ago, those who argued that the sanctity of life should prevail over capital punishment were in the minority. They may still be today. But rulings by both the California and the United States Supreme Courts in 1972 restricted the use of capital punishment. These rulings suggest that the sanctity of life may be taking on greater significance in the capital punishment controversy.

Changes in values over time can cause much consternation, especially as one grows older and, perhaps, more conservative. Conflicts over changes in value orientation frequently become obvious as part of the abrasiveness of the so-called "generation gap." The "gap" illustrates that value commitments change, for individuals and for the society, over time. It also illustrates the notion of *interpersonal* value conflict—that is, value conflicts that occur between individuals. Recall the capital punishment controversy again. One person argues in terms of the sanctity of human life, another in terms of the security of the community or the right to retribution. There is a conflict between the values being emphasized by the antagonists.

Note also, however, that a good deal of the consternation caused by shifts in value emphasis is due not to interpersonal value conflict (between, for example, parents and children), but to *intrapersonal* conflict—between different values held by one individual. The young are particularly likely to bring conflicting values in from the shadows of their elders' minds—making us aware of the dissonance that is latent in our value systems. One reason that barbs from young people evoke such strong responses is that they probe at the heart of their elders' psychological well-being. They threaten to bring to consciousness one's own early zeal for ideals that have not quite been abandoned.

How do we handle intrapersonal value conflict? The psychological manipulations (usually unconscious) that we use are commonly discussed in psychology texts. One is compartmentalization. We avoid the discomfort of inconsistency by maintaining neat, tight compartments in our minds. We may compartmentalize situations (a person who wouldn't steal money out of a cash register might steal towels from a motel, and not see any relationship between the two acts). We may compartmentalize values, which in essence means leaving one or more in the shadows of our mind (for example, by supporting an open housing law because it would enhance equality of opportunity, but neglecting to attend to the violation of property rights that might also occur).

Other psychological manipulations include discounting the importance of one of the conflicting elements ("Taking towels isn't really *that* big a deal!") *or* reducing the importance of the source of dissonance ("What does a young twirp [or a bearded hippie] like that know, anyhow?").

Of course, a person can also try to recognize his inconsistencies and handle them rationally. This is important in explicating one's own frame of reference in order to build a rationale for dealing with values as a teacher. The need to recognize and handle value conflicts should also be taken into account in deciding what the formal curriculum should attempt to teach students about values. Although discussions of "emergent" values, focusing on changes in values over time, have been fairly common in recent educational literature, less consideration has been given to the phenomenon of intrapersonal value conflict. But it is critical that educators pay attention to value conflict of this type.

The decisions teachers make often involve value conflicts. Value Exploration 3, p. 40, gives you the opportunity to reflect on the conflicts raised when a teacher is confronted by choices among moral values.

Is Value Conflict Normal?

A keystone is the recognition that value conflict is normal; it is not a sign of malformation, but an inevitable fact of life. This point was dramatically illustrated on the societal level by the title Gunnar Myrdal (1944) and his colleagues chose for their epic study of what was then referred to as "the Negro problem" in America. The title, *An American Dilemma*, epitomizes the consternation of a moralistic, rationalistic nation whose treatment of a large segment of its population did not (and still does not) square with its basic moral values. In Myrdal's words:

> . . . [O]ur problem is the moral dilemma of the American—the conflict between his moral valuations on various levels of consciousness and generality. The "American Dilemma," referred to in the title of this book,

is the ever-raging conflict between, on the one hand, the valuations preserved on the general plane which we shall call the "American Creed," where the American thinks, talks, and acts under the influence of high national and Christian precepts, and, on the other hand, the valuations on specific planes of individual and group living, where personal and local interests; economic, social and sexual jealousies; considerations of community prestige and conformity; group prejudice against particular persons or types of people; and all sorts of miscellaneous wants, impulses, and habits dominate his outlook (p. xlvii).

A man says he believes in equality of opportunity as a basic value; yet he hires no blacks in his factory or gives them only menial jobs (less likely to happen now with equal employment opportunity laws). Does this mean that equality of opportunity is *not* one of his values?

We often say that we can tell what a person values by how he acts. This is true. But the converse—that we can tell by the same acts what he does *not* value—is not true. The employer may value equality of opportunity, but he also has more specific values—the right to run his business as he pleases, the approbation of his neighbors. The pressures of his immediate environment will often make these relatively specific values more salient than a general value such as equality of opportunity, and the businessman acts in ways that belie his commitment to equality. But that does not mean that equality is not one of his values, any more than a man's decision to play poker means he doesn't value solitude, or his decision not to tell his wife that her new dress is hideous means that he does not value honesty. In the immediate situation, one value takes precedence over another. Of course, if a person declared that he valued equality of opportunity but *never* acted in ways consistent with that value, we would begin to doubt his commitment.

Myrdal emphasized the conflict between "moral valuations on various levels of consciousness and generality." In particular, he stressed the conflict between values on "the general plane" and the "specific planes of individual and group living." But it is essential to remember that as we attempt to apply our values to specific situations, conflict also occurs between values on the same level of generality—between personal preferences, between middle-level values, and between the basic values that are so fundamental to our conception of democracy and to which we have such strong commitments that Myrdal referred to them as the *American Creed*.

Value conflicts occur not only between moral values, but between esthetic and instrumental values as well. One esthetic value may conflict with another (for example, the soft sounds of Henry Mancini versus the hard rock of Black Sabbath in many homes); instrumental values may conflict (orderliness, set up as a criterion of classroom behavior in order to achieve certain learning goals, may be incompatible with the freedom of movement and expression deemed essential to the enhancement of creativity); and there will be conflicts between esthetic and instrumental values (the most effective way of doing something may not be the most pleasing esthetically, and vice versa).

And of course, esthetic and instrumental values conflict with moral ones. Arguments over where to place expressways in cities illustrate the first type of conflict: The "esthetically pleasing" solution of cutting through undesirable slum areas has come into direct confrontation with moral values involved in displacing low-income, often elderly residents. In schools, a conflict between instrumental and moral values has been created by hair and dress standards. The instrumental value (hair length, assumed to be instrumental to instructional goals) may conflict with "the natural right to 'liberty'" as well as "such basic values as the preservation of maximum individual choice, protection of minority sentiments, and appreciation for divergent lifestyles," according to the Alaska Supreme Court in its September 1972 ruling rejecting hair standards at a Fairbanks junior high school.

This last example illustrates an important point: When there is a conflict between a moral and an esthetic or an instrumental value, other things being equal, the moral value will usually carry the day.[8] Likewise, a

© 1974 United Feature Syndicate, Inc.

middle-level moral value will prevail over a personal preference, and a basic value will prevail over a middle-level one. This tendency to view the more general values as more compelling is implicit in our definition of levels of values. It undoubtedly explains our inclination to unwittingly convert esthetic and instrumental values to moral status. When we approve or condemn an action, we want to be on the strongest possible ground.

[8] "Other things being equal" is an important qualifier. Recall that on page 29, we pointed out that we sometimes give in to the pressures of the immediate situation and act in accordance with lower-level rather than basic moral values. In addition, this statement assumes an *awareness* of the higher value and its relevance to the situation. If the individual has compartmentalized (see page 28) and so doesn't see that the higher value is pertinent, he or she is less likely to act in accordance with it. Awareness of the higher value is even likely to counteract immediate pressures. This is one reason why attention to values in schooling is potentially so important. By making students more aware of basic moral values and how they relate to decisions, there is a good chance that we can improve the caliber of moral judgments by decreasing the impact of parochial pressures in contrast with basic democratic considerations. Myrdal (1944, pp. 1029–1030) suggests that the educational influences of mobility, the mass media, and schooling are having that effect on our society.

Recap

This chapter has discussed the nature of values. The term *value* was defined and distinguished from the terms *value judgment* and *attitude*. It was emphasized that values are both cognitive and affective, that they have both intellectual and emotional components. Rough categories of values—esthetic, instrumental, and moral—were elaborated, and it was proposed that moral values can be profitably thought of as falling along a continuum which ranges from personal preferences to basic moral standards. The inevitability of value conflict—both interpersonal and intrapersonal—was emphasized. The notion of intrapersonal conflict—its inevitability in our culture, and the uncomfortable psychological state caused by the recognition of value dissonance—is particularly important.

To build a rationale for dealing with values, the teacher must understand each of these distinctions and points. We have noted some of the ways in which they affect teaching decisions. But to a large extent this chapter on the nature of values has been laying the groundwork for the more specific discussion of values in the schools of a democratic society. We turn to the context of democracy in Chapter 3.

Value Exploration 2

A. If a teacher makes the following *factual claims* or *directives*, what might be the implicit *value judgments*?

Factual Claims or Directives	Implicit Value Judgment(s)
1. "This class is not putting forth the necessary effort to pass the exam."	*You students should work harder. Passing the exam is important. . . .*
2. "Let's brainstorm the question Judy has raised in her report."	*Judy's question is worth brainstorming. Discussion is good. . . .*
3. "If you have something to say, please raise your hand rather than just talking out!"	

4. "This paper, though potentially interesting, is not well organized."

_____
_____

5. "Donna is a creative and independent thinker who can handle advanced work."

_____
_____
_____

6. "Give your honest reactions to this unit; that is, specify what you liked and disliked most."

_____
_____
_____

7. "I see from my records that you've handed in only half the worksheets."

_____
_____
_____

8. "Hurry up and get those textbooks open or I'll give a pop quiz!"

_____
_____
_____

9. "Rick, I'm interested in your point of view here. Perhaps you might relate your thoughts to Linda's."

_____
_____
_____
_____

10. "These kids are so apathetic! I'm pulling my hair out trying to motivate them!"

_____
_____

B. If a teacher makes the following *value judgments*—either implicitly or explicitly—what might be the underlying *value* (or *values*)?

Value Judgment	Value(s)
1. Students should ask questions rather than simply absorb information.	*Involvement. Personal relevance.* . . . _____
2. Evaluation of student performance should be related to course objectives.	*Fairness. Rationality in instruction.* . . . _____
3. A teacher should attempt whenever possible to individualize instruction so that each student experiences success.	_____ _____ _____
4. Youngsters who do not complete their homework should not be allowed to go to recess.	_____ _____ _____

5. Each student should design his own course of study and means of evaluation. _____

6. Test grades should be posted on the bulletin board to motivate slower students and acknowledge the achievement of faster ones. _____

7. Students should be grouped according to ability. _____

8. Students should *not* be grouped according to ability. _____

9. Courses that deal with the concerns and heritage of minority groups should be added to the curriculum. _____

10. Our school should attempt to do more innovative things, such as modular scheduling and team teaching. _____

The Experiment

Problem *Identify the values that are perhaps being taught in the following situation.*

"So what do you think's going to happen?" Mr. Tiller asks with a trace of squint.

The room is bright as he lifts the glinting beaker, eyes it with purpose, and begins to tilt the pale acid, as if to answer his own question. Then he hesitates—

"Any ideas? What's your hypothesis based on the information you've got so far?"

The class is crowding around the demonstration table. "The tease," he thinks. "The trick is to set the hook." He puts the beaker down for a moment. He nods to a lanky fellow at the edge of the circle, mouthing an admonition to "hold it down" to some others. "One at a time," he says. The boy's face is smug and owly as he adjusts wire-framed glasses across the bridge of a freckled beak.

"I say it'll make carbon dioxide."

"How come?"

Hands are waving in Mr. Tiller's face.

"Uh, just the reaction," the boy shrugs. "I think it'll give off water and carbon dioxide."

"Uh-huh," Tiller nods in a noncommittal way. "How many agree with Allen?" A few hands go up; others are coming down.

"I think it's carbon dioxide *or* carbon monoxide," a hulking pigeon-browed girl is whining. "You can get either one. I mean, like it *depends*, you know?" Her eyes, spaced wide, are a blue glaze.

"Depends on what?" Mr. Tiller smiles.

"On the reaction," the girl sighs. "You can get either one."

The parabola of this circumlocution causes Mr. Tiller to blink. "I'm afraid I don't follow, Janice. What we've got to think of, you see, are principles of combining that might account for your theory. See if there's anything in the elements we're dealing with that would generate carbon monoxide or dioxide, okay?

"Any other theories?" Mr. Tiller asks.

"Nitrogen," one girl says.

"Hydrogen," a boy grins.

Mr. Tiller nods in a patient way. "Uh-huh. Tell me about the hydrogen theory, Curtis." He eyes the beaker again.

"Well, you mix the acid and the metal, see—"

"Oxygen," a girl offers.

The boy with the hydrogen theory thinks he is off the hook and lounges off to the right. Mr. Tiller picks up the beaker again. It is early in the year, and he rolls up the sleeve of his lab coat, baring his left arm. The students watch him finger a spattering of thin white scars.

"Here's what happens when you think chemistry is just messing around with chemicals," he says. "You see, I learned that it's probably a pretty good idea to do the experiment in your head before you do it in lab."

"Hey, *shrapnel*," one of the clowns guffaws.

"Of course, eyes don't heal like this," Mr. Tiller counters. "So maybe we'd better think through our theories a little more, okay?" Somewhere down the hall students are laughing and banging lockers.

"You see, science isn't just a guessing game," Mr. Tiller continues. "It's a way of behaving—a whole set of attitudes, if you know what I mean. It's a way of asking questions and making theories and gathering data to confirm or deny whatever your hunch is. Every theory has a *why* behind it."

A hand is up. "So what kind of gas does it make, Mr. Tiller?"

"Use your head on it, Cindy. Think it through."

"Uh, I'm sorry. I guess I need some help to get it."

"Well, maybe this will help," Mr. Tiller grins. He passes around a mimeographed sheet on which the apparatus for the experiment and the problem equation are laid out; then he nods to the boy with the hydrogen theory.

"Why don't you take it from here, Curtis? Go to work on that equation if you can."

In a moment or two their attention has been directed to the homework problem which no one has done, and students are arguing back and forth about how the equation will work. Mr. Tiller moderates and listens, asking a question now and then or clarifying the muddle with a point of information.

It seems incredible to him that having this kind of fun with a bunch of adolescents can actually be accepted as professional and a way of making a living. It is too *easy*, he thinks. All he does is listen for those places where kids have trouble understanding the topic under study; this is where his teaching or re-teaching begins. The main problem is helping them get over the fear of making mistakes.

A small, wild-haired boy off to Mr. Tiller's right is wrinkling his nose like a nearsighted mole. His name is Gunther and he's had nothing to say since the beginning of the semester. He is now fidgeting and staring at the beaker of acid.

"Any questions?" Mr. Tiller asks.

"Yeah," Gunther says. "We're going to bubble off some gas through water, right? But how do we *know* that the gas is what we think it is? I mean, it *could* be something else, if you follow what I'm saying. Everybody's just going on *faith* that this equation works like we've said it does and that the stuff Mr. Tiller's got is what he *says* it is." He narrows his eyes. "I mean, it seems to me we ought to be able to imagine some kind of experiment to *test* whatever we get coming off."

To Mr. Tiller, Gunther is talking science. He is crossing the line that distinguishes the experimental mind from the ordinary one. Here's a kid who'll be fun to have around for a semester.

"Hmmmmmmm," Mr. Tiller murmurs.

"Uh, if it's hydrogen it ought to burn," one of the quiet girls says. "There may be some other tests, I don't know."

"Let's talk about that for just a moment," Mr. Tiller says. He is having a good time as he watches notebooks click open. With luck, he suspects that they may even get to the experiment before the period is over.

Follow-up *What values does Mr. Tiller seem to have in mind? Can you distinguish the cognitive and affective elements? Is he doing a good job of teaching values?*

Esthetic Values over Tea and Crumpets

Problem *Whose views on esthetics and grading do you share?*

"Excuse me? Do you have a moment to chat?"

Mrs. Lawrence was smiling as I gathered a small cake into my napkin and tried to balance a shaky tea cup.

"Of course," I said.

In a few moments we were seated across from one another at one of the cafeteria tables. Mrs. Lawrence was a slender, personable woman in her late twenties—attractive, intelligent, and vice-president of the PTA. She was also mother of Todd Lawrence, a gabby, undisciplined youngster who sometimes gave me fits. Todd wasn't a "bad" child—I knew that—but he *was* physically and mentally immature.

"It's about Todd's work," Mrs. Lawrence said. "From your comments on his coloring work and penmanship exercises, I take it that he's not doing very well."

"Well, Todd *is* having some problems," I admitted. "In the area of neatness and following directions he seems to have a little more difficulty than most students. I think we just have to be patient with him."

"I'm glad to hear you say that," Mrs. Lawrence said. "That's *precisely* my feeling. I know that Todd isn't an angel and I know that he's not as coordinated as he might be. What I've had some trouble understanding, though, is why you should criticize the *form* of his work the way you have—I mean, with 'happy faces' and 'sad faces.' "

"Well, I'm simply trying to get Todd to do his best," I said. "Even though he may be immature, he needs to learn what's expected of him. If he gets the idea that sloppy work is acceptable, he'll have problems all the way through school." I tasted the crumbly, warm cake.

Mrs. Lawrence tried to smile, but her mouth was tight. "I'd feel better," she said, "if you wouldn't put those 'sad faces' on Todd's papers—even if he *does* go outside the lines."

My stomach knotted slightly. "I see." I touched my napkin to my lips.

"After all, we *do* have to be patient with him, don't we?"

"Yes, I think we do," I said. "But tell me: Don't you agree that good handwriting, neatness, and attractive looking papers are worthwhile things for Todd to work at?"

"Frankly, I'm not so sure," Mrs. Lawrence answered after a pause. "When we focus all our attention on neatness—on penmanship and margins and staying in the lines—we forget what the child is actually *saying* in his composition or drawing. Perhaps his coloring work isn't so good in your eyes, but *I* think it's very creative at times. In fact, I'd like to see Todd *experiment* with color—to go outside the lines whenever he feels like it. I'd like to see him make his letters in whatever way comes natural to him."

"We have to have a certain amount of discipline," I said. "Naturalness may be good, but. . . ."

"But do we have to make the children into conformists?" Mrs. Lawrence asked.

Follow-up *Continue the dialog in your mind. Try to answer Mrs. Lawrence's question.*

Find another person who has also read the conversation up to the point where it stops. Role-play the situation to see where it takes each of you in an exploration of your esthetic values. Then switch roles.

In your opinion, is it fair for teachers to give grades on esthetic criteria such as form, neatness, and penmanship? If so, under what circumstances? Should esthetic criteria be separated from other criteria—for example, the "content" of an in-class essay?

Instrumental Values, Kids, and Potted Plants

Problem *How much "order" is necessary to have a productive classroom?*

I guess I had the first ominous twinge about student teaching on the morning I met my cooperating teacher. She was a tall, heavy-set woman in her late forties, and she was busily at work lining up desks along the gray and white tile lines. The students had just been dismissed for lunch.

"These kids," she sighed. "Sometimes I think they're nothing but *wild animals.* Just *look* at this mess they leave!"

I blinked and tried to find the mess. What I saw were even rows of desks and books neatly shelved. Mrs. Ashcroft's potted plants were lined like sentries along the window ledge, flanked by two printed signs that read "Do Not Touch." She picked up a scrap of paper and shelved a dictionary. *"There,"* she said. "That's better."

I soon discovered that Mrs. Ashcroft's universe was one where everything—and everyone—had its place. Her gradebook, her desk, her time schedule—all were laid out with care and precision. Each student knew the schedule of activities and understood that this schedule was fixed, unchanging; each knew the specific place for various kinds of assignments, the deadlines, the procedures for makeup work, and the penalties for failing to observe manuscript conventions; each knew that the program of study moved straight through the text, lesson by lesson, and that questions not pertinent to the current reading upset Mrs. Ashcroft.

About a week after I had that first twinge of uneasiness, Mrs. Ashcroft and I had a talk about my ideas for student teaching. I had submitted a unit plan to her, and we were going over it.

"About this group work," she said. "I think you'll find that youngsters take advantage of that kind of situation. They need a very definite structure, you see. And I think you'll find that they do better and *like* it better if they move along at the same rate. That makes things easier to manage, too."

I chose my words with care. "Well, I'm hoping to provide some structure *in* the groups," I said. "Each group will have a chairman, and. . . ."

"That's good in theory," Mrs. Ashcroft interrupted. "But it's difficult to maintain a good work atmosphere with a lot of confusion. These youngsters definitely need a sense of order—they need things laid out for them. If you let the students start going off in all directions, you have chaos and discipline problems. Your job is to control and *teach* these youngsters, not run a circus."

"I definitely don't want a circus," I murmured. "What I want is to promote involvement. I know that some groups will need to have things laid out for them, but I'm also hoping that some youngsters will get involved and do more than just enough to get by."

Mrs. Ashcroft shook her head. A small sigh escaped between her teeth as she looked at the plants again. "I don't see how you expect to keep track of all this," she said. "You'll have kids all over the room, working on different levels."

"I'm willing to give it a try." I winked, testing a grin on her.

Mrs. Ashcroft didn't smile back. "And because you can't plan this kind of program out in advance," she added, "it's bound to be disorganized and chaotic. I'm afraid it will be a bad experience for the students."

Silence.

"I know that all the details haven't been nailed down," I admitted. "It just seems to me that the students will be more likely to learn if they have a say in *some* of the directions we take."

Mrs. Ashcroft turned to the window ledge. "After all, you don't ask the plants whether they *need* water. It's your job—your responsibility—to provide what they need."

I closed my planning book and looked Mrs. Ashcroft in the eye. "We certainly see things differently," I said.

Follow-up *What instrumental values seem to govern Mrs. Ashcroft's point of view? What are the instrumental values of the student teacher?*

Assume that you are the student teacher in this situation. What would you be inclined to do? Argue? Attempt to effect a compromise? Give up? Role-play the conversation with a friend to sort out your instrumental values and resolve the conflict.

Moral Values and the "Teacher-Counselor"

Problem *What moral values should guide the teacher's behavior?*

It's inevitable. Different teachers attract different kinds of youngsters. And for some reason I seem to attract the shy ones. Maybe it's because I'm rather quiet myself and can understand how it is when you'd rather not talk up in front of a group or share your problems and feelings with just anyone.

In any case, I was in the habit of staying around after school—and I tried to communicate to my students that they were welcome to drop by any time. No big thing, really. I was just there—correcting papers and planning and talking to whoever wanted to talk. I think they can tell if you're there to listen or if you're just waiting for a ride. So I tried to be around, and I tried to listen.

I had perhaps half a dozen regular visitors to my after-school "class," plus occasional "strays." Sometimes they'd come to do homework, sometimes to chat, sometimes to look at the magazine rack, sometimes to horse around—and sometimes to harass me. It was really sort of nice. But a little scary, you know? Sometimes kids will lay some pretty heavy stuff on you if you let them see you're interested in them as human beings.

I was just about ready to go home the afternoon Ilene came by. She's a quiet little sophomore—sensitive, pretty, a beautiful smile. We were gossiping about nothing in particular, and I remember I had just asked her about the plaid jumper she was wearing because I was interested in getting the pattern from a fabric shop on the way home. There was a slight pause as if she were catching her breath. I just waited without saying anything and smiled at her. That was all it took, I guess, because she looked at me and then put her head down on the desk top and began sobbing.

She was two months pregnant. And she was scared because she was only fifteen years old, and her boyfriend was just seventeen. She knew that her parents were going to "go through the roof" if they found out. I suggested that "if" would probably have to be changed to "when." It was then that I found out that she and the boy were talking about running away—which, in her opinion, was better than facing up to her folks.

Since I didn't know exactly what to do, I said something about talking to the Girls' Counselor. Ilene just started to cry again, harder this time. Her parents and the other kids would find out for sure, she said, and if that happened, she'd run away by herself, especially if I betrayed her. That really put me on the spot. Then she wanted to know if I knew where she could get an abortion. I'll have to admit I didn't know what to say for a moment.

Follow-up *What would you do? List the short-range and long-range alternatives that you can think of. Then list the moral values that would justify the alternatives you've identified. Check your lists against those of others in your class.*

A. Short-range Alternatives	Values Supported	B. Long-range Alternatives	Values Supported

Value Exploration 3

Turn again to "Moral Values and the 'Teacher-Counselor' " (p. 38). Think about your answers to the "Follow-up." Which short- and long-range alternatives would you choose? Which values would you be supporting?

Would you have made the same choice four years ago? Might you make a different choice ten years from now?

Would your parents have made the same choice? If not, what value (or values) would they emphasize? Or think of some other significant person in your life who might disagree with your choice of alternatives. What different value or values would that person probably want to support?

Look at the values that support the alternatives you did not choose. Are any of these values unimportant to you? Are you sure that these values are not as significant to you as the ones that support the short- and long-range alternatives you chose?

Finally, think of another situation, perhaps one in which you were personally involved as a student, in which a teacher made an important ethical judgment that affected you. (Perhaps it was a judgment involving grades or discipline, or even something that happened out of school.) Identify the interpersonal value conflicts (perhaps between you and the teacher, or between the teacher and someone else, such as the principal or your parents). Then identify the intrapersonal value conflicts that could have occurred for you and for the teacher.

The Democratic Context

What, you might ask, is a book that purports to be about values and teaching in general, not just about social studies, doing with a chapter on democracy? After all, social studies teachers and curriculum developers are the ones who take responsibility for citizenship education aren't they? So, aren't they the only ones who need to be concerned with such things as the meaning of democracy?

Of course, it is not true that social studies teachers are the only ones concerned with citizenship. Social studies teachers are particularly concerned with preparing students to be "good" political citizens. But most teachers, regardless of their teaching area, profess some interest in citizenship as an educational goal. Training for citizenship, or at least for proper deportment, is usually considered to be a function of the total school.

But a teacher has other reasons to contemplate the meaning of democracy. The school, as a formal educational institution, is a creature of the society it serves. As teachers in the school, we are agents of that society.[1] This fact has complex and far-reaching implications for us. It is vital that each teacher have a clear conception of democracy, for this is a critical part of an adequate rationale for dealing with values in the school. Your conception of democracy will influence your decisions about what values to treat and how to treat them, as well as help or hinder you in justifying your decisions to parents and administrators.

What follows is a sketching of some value-related assumptions about the society which employs us to teach. Read and criticize. Above all, ask whether the view of democracy laid out here coincides with your own, and if not, which perspective provides the more adequate framework for deciding what you as a teacher should do about values.

---

[1] That is, of the *society*, not of the *establishment*. The major premise of this book is that each teacher needs to be clear about his or her role as an agent of a *democratic society*, not of whatever economic, racial, ethnic, and/or religious group is currently in power.

Defining Democracy

We assume that most people will agree that our society is a democracy—at least in intent, if not always in actuality. Democracy is commonly defined as a society which is governed by the majority. The Greek *demokratia* and the New England town meeting are often cited as examples, with an ideal of direct participation by the citizen in mind. But ideals and reality frequently differ. In neither the Greek *demokratia* or the New England town meeting did all of the citizens have the will or the opportunity to participate. In each case unelected representatives made the decisions.

Our modern form of government, called a *republic,* is a response to the obvious impossibility of bringing large masses of people together to make laws. It fits the majority rule definition of democracy by providing elections as the mechanism whereby a majority of concerned citizens can select governmental representatives and subject them to periodic review. When votes are taken in legislative and judicial bodies, decisions are also by majority rule.

This popular definition of democracy—that is, democracy as majority rule—is the source of many complaints about "undemocratic" actions by the government. People find fault, for example, with court decisions that limit prayer in the classroom because "the majority wants prayer, and in a democracy, the will of the majority should be followed."

But what if a national plebiscite were held on the question: "Should all Mormons be executed?"—and a distinct majority voted "yes"?[2] Would we say that this was clearly a democratic decision, that the government should execute Mormons because it was mandated to do so by a majority vote? Undoubtedly not!

As a matter of fact, even taking such a vote would be considered an unthinkable heresy to the democratic faith. There would be an immediate outcry, and not only from the group threatened with extinction. For democracy involves more than majority rule. Protection of the rights of individuals and minorities is also essential. (Ironically, many people who argue vociferously for prayer in the schools on the basis of majority rule—even though some minorities claim that such prayer violates their right to religious freedom—would be strident in opposing the persecution of a religious minority, especially one to which they belonged. This is a good example of value conflict and the shifting of value emphasis as the pinching shoe shifts feet.)

[2] This example is salient for a person living in Utah, Mormon or non-Mormon. Substitute the name of any religious, ethnic, or other minority group that is more meaningful, i.e., evokes more emotional reaction, for you.

But why majority rule, and why protect minority rights? An adequate answer is one that justifies and integrates majority rule and minority rights in a definition of democracy. One plausible approach to such a definition is suggested by the responses that could be anticipated to the somewhat facetious suggestion above that a vote be taken on genocide. "It would be inhumane." "You just don't treat humans that way." Implicit in such reactions is an ideal of human-ness—that being human is of itself important and demands respect. This belief that each individual has worth and deserves consideration because he is human—and equal to anyone else in that sense, if not in wealth, intellect, or physical prowess—is, we believe, central to democracy.[3] Its essence is captured in the phrase *human dignity.* It is this central democratic value from which the values of majority rule and minority rights are derived and to which they contribute.

Our history is that a group of idealists back at the beginning of our Republic created an ideology of democracy based on the premise that all men are created equal. That is the same as creating a form of mathematics based on certain tables of addition, multiplication, and subtraction. These are stated as truths, against which there is no argument or the system will not work. The same holds true with both democracy and mathematics. . . .

For purposes of conducting a democracy it is not necessary that the people be proved equal. It is only necessary that they maintain equality by common assent.

Therefore, and quite obviously, the basic issue does not concern Negroes as a race, but is concerned only with the question whether democracy is an acceptable ideology to the majority of citizens.

—Chester Himes. *Black on Black*, 1973.

Majority rule, for example, is not just a chance occurrence in the development of democratic political institutions. It directly reflects an emphasis upon equality which is inherent in the ideal of individual dignity. When the votes of those who have equal dignity are being weighed, the scale shifts according to the number of votes on each side, not according to *who* cast them.

The emphasis placed by the ideal of human dignity upon the worth of each individual also provides the basis for individual and minority rights in a

---

[3] Michael Scriven (1966) uses the notion of equal rights, in the sense of equal consideration, as the basis for a democratic ethic. His work suggests another way to construe the democratic context for schooling. However, it should be noted that Scriven's ideal of equality and the ideal of human dignity, as defined here, are closely related (see, for example, Oliver & Shaver, 1966, pp. 46–48).

democracy. The right to life, liberty, and the pursuit of happiness, to freedom from despotic government, to freedom of speech, press, and religion, to due process of law, and to equal protection of the law—these rights, as spelled out in our fundamental political documents, are values essential to the definition of human dignity in this society. And so are others, such as the right to shelter and to freedom from hunger added during the Great Depression; the right to domestic tranquility (law and order); the right to responsibility (rationality). That is, it is commonly accepted that protection of these values—the principles of the American Creed—enhances the dignity of individuals in our society.

It is important to note that the basic democratic rights are values. They are principles or standards by which we judge the morality of individual, collective, and governmental actions. But when we think of democratic values, we must go beyond rights. Such values as domestic tranquility (a reasonably stable existence) and responsibility (often over-looked by young people who see their rights violated but are not ready to take full responsibility for their own actions and well-being) are also extensions of, and essential to, human dignity.

The classroom crackles with tension. A rebel youngster has challenged you. "We voted on this thing. I thought we had majority rule!" Do the ideas in this chapter apply to the classroom? See "Mini-Democracy in Room 16," p. 44.

Basic Instrumental Values

Although the values in the democratic ethos—the American Creed—are obviously basic moral values, they also function as instrumental values.[4] They do so in two related senses. (1) Values such as due process of law, especially as interpreted by the courts, provide procedural guidelines for governmental officials. (2) Preserving each of the values in the Creed helps to maintain the broader concept of dignity.

Let's consider the value of freedom of speech to illustrate these two points. Court interpretations of the meaning of freedom of speech provide standards for officials who must make such decisions as whether to allow the use of loudspeakers on cars for political announcements; or whether to issue permits for various types of rallies. Also, when the policies and actions of government officials (and private citizens) are judged by, and forced toward the criterion of, free speech, it is more difficult for these same officials to deny human dignity in other matters. In an environment of free

[4] See Chapter 2, pages 20–22.

speech, which includes protection for people who speak out against the government, violations of other basic values are less likely. Freedom of speech (and press) makes it probable both that such violations will be made known, and that proposed or present policies will be openly debated in terms of the values they may violate.

Here's what Franklin D. Roosevelt, 32nd President of the United States, said about the importance of a free press:

> "Freedom of conscience, of education, of speech, of assembly are among the very foundations of democracy and all of them would be nullified should freedom of the press ever be successfully challenged."

And so for all of the basic democratic values. Each is an important end in itself in our society; and each helps to define and maintain the conception of dignity that is so central to a democracy. But, as we emphasized in Chapter 2, the basic values in the Creed conflict with one another by their very nature.

Application of particular values to concrete situations reveals the incompatibilities. Conflicts occur between individual and minority rights (as between freedom of association and equal protection of the law, in cases of racial or religious segregation). Conflicts occur between individual or minority rights and societal values such as majority rule (as in the classroom prayer dispute) and domestic stability–values that are also rooted in the ideal of dignity.[5]

This inherent conflict means that we cannot fully attain all of the basic values at any one time. As we move toward full attainment of one, we inevitably will have to compromise another. Hence the major continuing policy question that underlies so much political and social controversy:

[5] It is worth noting that the conflict between majority rule and individual-minority rights is built into our governmental system. Two branches of the government—the executive and legislative—rest on electoral bases that force them to reflect (or to try to give the impression of reflecting) the democratic concern for majority rule. One branch, the judiciary, was established to protect the individual and minority rights that are also fundamental to our conception of democracy. That is a basic reason why judges are not elected. The United States Supreme Court in particular, with its function of ultimate review of constitutional questions, finds itself dealing with disputes involving the basic rights of individuals and minorities. When it fulfills its obligation and on occasion rules against the "majority," the Court finds itself subjected to criticism that often reaches an incredibly vituperative level. (Dahl, 1958, has suggested that there is no evidence to prove that the Supreme Court has frequently gone against the wishes of the majority. Instead, extremely vocal minorities cry out so loudly that it sounds as though a majority has been affronted.) By the very nature of their attacks—vilifying the Court for acting contrary to what they assume the wishes of the majority to be—the critics frequently evidence an unfortunate shallowness of understanding of the relationship of the courts to the democratic ethos, and of the conflicting nature of our basic values.

What blend of the conflicting basic values should we support in order to achieve optimal dignity for every member of our society? It is critical that you be aware of this problem. It will help you to avoid treating basic values in a way that leads students to have unrealistic expectations. And it may help you to counteract the cynicism of students who see ideals go unfulfilled and conclude that this lack of fulfillment reflects only the evil in people.

Last week, for the first time, the Supreme Court publicly grappled with the sensitive, divisive issue of preferential admissions policies for minority-group college students. . . .

The case was brought by Marco DeFunis, Jr., a white student who claimed that the University of Washington unconstitutionally discriminated against him by refusing him admission to law school while accepting 36 minority-group students with lower academic qualifications. . . .

The case was a conflict between two cherished popular notions—the idea that minorities discriminated against in the past should have special help to overcome the effects of past inferior treatment and the notion that everyone should be judged on his own merits.

[DeFunis' attorney argued that] "The failure to consider all applicants on an equal basis was a denial of the equal protection of the laws . . . [and that the University] . . . had demonstrated no 'overriding public interest' in . . . admitting some minority students with 'lower grades and qualifications'. . . ."

— The Chronicle of Higher Education, March 4, 1974.

Can you state the values underlying the two "popular notions" mentioned above? Are "equal protection of the law" and "public interest" basic values?

Human Dignity and Intelligence

Another aspect of human dignity is critical to a consideration of the school's educational function, especially vis-à-vis values. It is the ideal of man as an autonomous, intelligent being, on both a personal and a societal level. The democratic ideal is not that of a man completely free to do as he wishes. Nor is it that of an unfeeling, unemotional, totally rational being. Rather, the ideal of human dignity implies that each individual has the right to self-fulfillment, to make the major decisions about his own destiny, and that emotion and commitment will be tempered by intelligent reflection in the decision-making process.

So a democratic society is committed to intelligence and to the right to choose as essential ingredients of humanness. In addition, it is committed to the belief that intellectual abilities can be improved, even if they cannot be perfected. The implications for teachers are important, for the public generally assumes that the improvement of decision-making capabilities lies within the school's legitimate domain.

Clearly, parents accept formalized thinking skills—such as in mathematics—as within the school's instructional prerogatives. Problems arise when teachers attempt to move beyond the boundaries of formal subject matter into the cultivation of thinking for everyday life. As John Dewey (1916, p. 148) noted, thinking involves risk. When you encourage students to think, the end product cannot be guaranteed, and it may deviate substantially from what parents would like. Trying to improve the thinking skills of young people, in order to enhance their dignity, can therefore be dangerous.

It's 7:10 A.M. You're leisurely sipping orange juice and scanning the "Letters to the Editor" in the morning newspaper. You're hoping to find some juicy items for class discussion. Then, suddenly, you're trembling with a sick feeling—a mixture of anger and fear. See "Devil's Advocate," p. 60, for more details.

School people who seriously attempt to teach their students to apply their intelligence outside narrow academic limits are often severely criticized. This ironic state of affairs becomes understandable if we recall the conflicting nature of values and add the nature of a pluralistic society. It is important to understand how values and pluralism are interrelated. This will help you to build a rationale that can protect you against being trapped and penalized by the paradoxes of the society you serve as a teacher.

Pluralism—A Sine Qua Non of Democracy

It is not uncommon to hear people refer to some nations as monolithic societies—especially communist nations like the U.S.S.R. and the People's Republic of China. The narrow application of this term to nations containing millions of people is absurd. Consider the variety of backgrounds and experiences that people have in different geographical regions and different socio-economic strata, even in China! It is difficult to believe that if it were possible to become closely acquainted with many individuals in any society, one would find "massive uniformity." Certainly it does not exist even in small communities that provide less opportunity for diversity—for example, rural Mormon communities in Utah, black neighborhoods in South

Chicago, and "advantaged" plush suburbs east of Los Angeles. The surface appearance of monolithism disappears as one gets to know the residents.

Yet there is a certain sense in which it is meaningful to talk about monolithic societies, especially where there is a determined drive toward uniformity. In some national and local communities there are strong, frequently conscious, efforts to subjugate individual differences to one predominant doctrine, whether political (as in Russia or Red China) or religious (as in Utah). Such communities demand uniformity on doctrinal issues, especially as interpreted and propounded by political or religious authorities. The result is often considerable homogeneity—at least on the surface for public view. This is especially true when there is little influx of new ideas because dissemination is controlled by the authorities or because few new people join the community.

It makes sense to describe such societies as monolithic, especially when they are contrasted with pluralistic societies. While the monolithic society attempts to make its members feel that their affiliation with one dominant group should be *the* determining influence on their lives, the pluralistic society encourages, or at least openly tolerates, a multiplicity of groups. Members of the society see this pluralism as a positive attribute. They accept the diversity of ideas that are expressed as a result, and they protect the expression of these ideas (even if with misgivings at times).

This diversity can be difficult to accept in concrete situations where the ideas expressed are viewed as radical, as was the case with early opposition to U.S. involvement in Vietnam. For that reason, institutionalized protections, such as our commitment to freedom of speech and our judicial system, are vital. Most important, however, is the democratic commitment to a process of rational consent in decision making. It provides the context for expression of opinion, for exercise of persuasion and reason, and finally for abiding by decisions reached via legitimate procedures.

Teachers would often be well advised to consider whether they treat unconventional students in ways consistent with human dignity and the assumed benefits of pluralism. School people also need to reflect on the validity of students' complaints (which the courts have agreed to on occasion) that our schools do not adequately protect the expression of divergence, and thus lose the benefits of pluralism for education.

What is so great about pluralism? To begin with, diversity is interesting—it is boring to be surrounded by people who are all alike. But it would be trite to suggest that avoiding dreary monotony is the basic justification for pluralism. On the contrary, the assumed benefits of a pluralistic society are fundamental to democracy; and, as noted above, pluralism and basic values such as freedom of speech and press go hand in hand.

The pressure of diverse views in the community, and the provision of the means to express them, serve fundamental functions. In many situations, latent problems, overlooked by people with similar outlooks on life, are identified by the person whose outlook is different. When a newcomer raises questions about the treatment of minority groups in a community which "has no minority problem," or a student challenges long-standing procedures in your classroom, the consternation that is created may be unwelcome—but it often throws the decision-making process into motion. Moreover, once problems are posed, diversity of opinion makes it likely that a broad range of options will be available from which to work out solutions. Diversity, and controversy based on diversity, can even be the catalyst for a rejuvenation of commitments. Clashes with those of unlike mind can force people to reconsider the meanings of their values and the reasonableness of their priorities—as college students proved in the late sixties.

. . . If there is no struggle, there is no progress. Those who profess to favor freedom, and yet depreciate agitation, are men who want crops without plowing up the ground. They want rain without thunder and lightning. They want the ocean without the awful roar of its many waters. . . .

—Frederick Douglass

These contributions to the decision-making process, and not just dissent for its own sake, were undoubtedly what Supreme Court Justice William O. Douglas had in mind when he commented: "I don't know of any salvation for society except through eccentrics, misfits, dissenters, people who protest."

Without a variety of openly expressed views, decision making is meaningless, an empty exercise. In monolithic societies, regardless of the form it takes, decision making is a sham because the problems to be dealt with, and frequently the decisions to be made, are prescribed before the process begins. For that reason, pluralism is a *sine qua non* of democracy. Real opportunities for decision making are an essential aspect of the core concept of human dignity.

This emphasis on the contribution of divergent points of view may seem uncalled for, a belaboring of the obvious. But the concept of pluralism should be central to your hidden curriculum decisions as you interact with students, and to your decisions about how to deal with values in the formal curriculum. People often fail to appreciate the importance of pluralism, and diversity, when they are faced with specific situations. The results of the National Assessment of Educational Progress (1970) illustrate this, and confirm the findings of earlier polls. When knowledge and attitudes related to citizenship education were assessed, the freedom to express unpopular opinions was the "least understood or valued" of the Constitutional rights (pp. 28–29, 35). People were asked whether three statements should be allowed on radio or television. One statement said that Russia was better than the United States; one that some races of people are better than others; and one that it is not necessary to believe in God. The results suggest how difficult it is for people to support the expression of ideas they disagree with. Ninety-four percent of the thirteen-year-olds, 78% of the seventeen-year-olds, and 68% of the adults answered No. And of those who said the statements should be allowed, only 3 percent, 17 percent, and 24 percent respectively cited the civic value of freedom of speech as a reason (pp. 28–29, 34–35). Such findings, which are not unique, merit attention whenever school people consider whether schools are fulfilling their obligations to a democratic society.

The United States is a multi-cultural society of considerable diversity, containing various ethnic groups, social-class subcultures, rural and urban subcultures, and a distinctive youth subculture, all of which vary in characteristics (i.e., emphases in language, thought, behavior, and values). The educational system, however, is largely mono-cultural; teaching proceeds within the cultural and linguistic framework of the dominant group. . . .

Instead of the "melting pot" objective of blending divergent groups into a single homogeneous mass, the objective should be to develop a "tossed salad" of different cultures and life styles, enhancing the values and uniqueness of each culture, so that, taken together, they become complementary. In other words, the objective should be to prepare people to live in a pluralistic society. This goal obviously goes beyond merely dealing with language differences or making minor accommodations in the system.

—D. C. Clement, P. A. Johnson, Glen Nimnicht, and James Johnson. *Beyond "Compensatory Education,"* 1973.

The National Assessment findings also confirm what others have found: Awareness of the importance of diversity increases somewhat with age and education. So the results indicating lack of acceptance of unpopular opinions do not necessarily represent the beliefs of prospective and practicing teachers. Nevertheless, the indicated lack of tolerance for the expression of divergent ideas in concrete situations suggests that it is important for each teacher to consider specifically the impact as well as the contributions of pluralism in developing a rationale from which to explain his or her behavior to parents and administrators.

Such considerations may also help you to appreciate the point of view of minority group parents who object to what they call the "white, middle-class" orientation of our schools. You may also be better able to understand and appreciate why some educators are calling for a change from the "melting pot" conception of the role of education to a "tossed salad" conception—one that emphasizes the distinctiveness and the various contributions of different subcultures and life styles. But if your rationale is to be adequate, it must also take into account explicitly the paradoxical role of values in promoting conflict and cohesion in a pluralistic society.

Money. There's nothing like it to bring out differences in human values. Read "Chicano Maverick," p. 62, to see how $88.50 raises a real problem—as well as an opportunity for value clarification.

Stresses and Strains

Pluralism is not all honey and cream. Diversity creates societal stresses, as has been obvious in recent years. And the divisive elements in a society have their impact on the schools that serve it. Pluralism means, for example, that school people are confronted with competing points of view about the proper role of the school. Under these conditions, it is not easy for a teacher to determine what his or her mandate is in regard to the teaching of values. This is especially true when the teacher is aware of the inevitable influence of his or her own frame of reference, and wants to make decisions that are more than affirmations of the prejudices and biases of the particular groups to which he or she happens to belong.

Which brings us directly back to our earlier comment that it is important to understand how values and pluralism are interrelated. You will need to understand this to cope with the competing pressures you will face as a teacher, and to decide how to deal with values as a teacher in a democratic society.

We have already noted that *intra*personal value conflict exists, due to inherent inconsistencies within individual sets of commitments. Inherent value inconsistencies and the differences in frames of reference that reflect a pluralistic society combine to contribute to *inter*personal value conflict. This is true of esthetic, instrumental, and moral values. But your conception of the nature and role of the basic moral values of our society is so critical to your value-related decisions as a teacher that it merits special consideration.

Values: Source of Conflict and Cohesion

We have seen that values are both cognitive and affective—that is, they have intellectual meaning and they arouse feelings. In fact, it makes sense to say that value terms—such as freedom of speech—have *descriptive meaning* (the cognitive concept that the term represents) and *emotive meaning* (the feelings aroused by the term) (Shaver & Larkins, 1973, pp. 205–206). This distinction becomes particularly important in considering the vagueness of value terms.

Vagueness and Conflict The basic values of our society are vague with respect to their descriptive meanings—a very important source of controversy and conflict. When a value is applied as a criterion for judging a specific situation or policy (for example, in deciding whether student protest groups should be allowed to use four-letter words on their signs), the descriptive meaning of the value term must be explicated. Otherwise, it is impossible to decide rationally whether the behavior or policy in question fits or violates the value criterion.

As descriptive meaning is specified, differences in the way people construe a value term become apparent. The descriptive meaning people give value terms is a function of the different experiences, and, consequently, the different frames of reference, that are encouraged in a pluralistic society. Conflict is the result.[6]

Students on the Berkeley campus used four-letter words a few years ago, at least ostensibly, to provoke people to think about what they took to be our society's indifference to the killing of civilians in Vietnam. Some people saw the students' signs and chants as outrageous insults. Others saw them as a legitimate use of symbols in an attempt to jar people into thinking about moral issues.

Obviously, whether a person viewed the "filthy speech movement" as falling within or outside the realm of freedom of speech—and thus as either justified or unjustified—depended on that person's frame of reference. The differences in experience that lead people to disagree over such vital questions are an interesting area for speculation, but one that is outside the scope of this book. What is relevant here is that teachers need to recognize that such disagreements are inevitable and legitimate in a pluralistic society. Therefore, you will need to reckon with them in your decisions about the formal and hidden curricula, as well as when you deal with parents.

---

[6] Note that the courts have been given the ultimate responsibility for providing authoritative definitions of disputed legal-value terms. Again, the nature of the task assigned them has embroiled the courts in heated controversy and opened them to vituperative attack.

Cohesion When people differ over the descriptive meaning of values and over which values to emphasize at any particular point in time, conflicts result. These conflicts are so obvious and so pervasive that they lead some people to conclude that there really is no such thing as an American Creed—no set of basic values to which all Americans tend to be committed. These people are correct in one important sense: *There probably is no one set of values which has the same descriptive meaning for all Americans.*

Yet, in another vital sense, the challengers are wrong. That is, *at the affective, emotional, level there is a commonality of commitment to a set of values that allows us to speak of an American Creed.* The very vagueness in descriptive meaning that underlies so much controversy allows the widely divergent groups in our society to hold common affective commitments to the basic values. Individuals across the nation can and do have common "good" feelings about values such as freedom of speech—the "rights of Americans"—even though they assign these values different descriptive meanings and different priorities.

We have noted that when people attempt to translate the basic values into social policies, or use them to judge specific actions, the disparities in descriptive meaning become obvious. It is important to note that, even then, persons who oppose a policy or action that others support in the name of a basic value rarely reject the value itself. Rather, they either argue that the value has been misdefined or they use other basic values to support their own position. When supporters of the "filthy speech movement" defended it in the name of free speech, its opponents argued, not that free speech was wrong, but that the use of four-letter words did not fall within the meaning of free speech. They also contended that the movement violated other basic values, such as majority rule (preserving the speech standards and sensitivities of the majority) and law and order (they argued that the use of "filthy speech" was a flagrant violation of antiobscenity laws and a possible provocation to violence by those offended).

The Creed and Cohesion

The contention that there is an American Creed that carries a common emotional meaning is no trivial matter. People who travel throughout our country are frequently impressed by the vast geographic territory and the tremendous subcultural differences. They find it remarkable that somehow, despite all these differences and divisive forces, the nation holds together.

What is the binding force? Is there something beyond the pervasive concern with economic welfare—middle-class materialism and financial security—which links the variety of subgroups in this society? Gunnar Myrdal concluded, "It is difficult to avoid the judgment that this 'American Creed' is the cement in the structure of this great and disparate nation" (p. 3).[7]

Common emotive commitments are critical to the cohesiveness of any society. Anthropologists pinpoint the nonintellectual nature of this aspect of culture when they refer to it as "projective reality." [8] It is a framework that the society's members take for granted as a context for thought, discussion, and action. In that sense, the American Creed is important in much the same way as a religious faith—not because its truth has been verified scientifically, but because it is accepted as part of the "natural" order of things.

The "cement" of a creed is especially vital to a pluralistic society with its emphasis on diversity and personal freedom. The emotive force of the ideals in the Creed provides a context for interaction that is often implicit, sometimes explicit, rarely questioned. It provides a common bond between, and a basis for confrontation and debate among, those with contending points of view.

"Everyone needs goals, something in life to strive for. You know, getting ahead, being someone. . . ."

Oh, do they? The lack of shared commitments can get in the way of classroom problem solving, too. See "The Problem," p. 63.

Have you ever tried to have a reasonable, productive argument geared toward solving a problem with someone who did not share your values—that is, not someone who emphasized values differently than you did, but who argued from a *different set* of values? Under those conditions, arguments about what is proper pass one another by without effect. To meet head-on, they must come from common value premises. Shared commitments are the basis for intelligent confrontation—even when the dispute involves which values are most important or how to translate them into policy and action.

[7] For an excellent discussion of the Creed and its historical roots, see Myrdal's (1944) Chapter 1, "American Ideals and the American Conscience."

[8] This term is used by Donald Oliver (1960, p. 212) in an excellent discussion of the dilemma of diversity and cohesion in a pluralistic society.

Potential Objections to the Creed in a Teaching Rationale

Awareness of the cohesive function of our society's basic values is a vital aspect of an adequate teaching rationale. However, there are two potential objections to this conception of a Creed. These objections need to be anticipated and dealt with.

The International Scene

If a conception of values is to provide an adequate basis for your teaching decisions, it must take into account the fundamental fact that the United States is part of a world community. The role of the nation-state in this era of high speed travel and communication is not yet clear. World government does not seem any closer to reality than it was at the end of World War II; yet there is a growing consciousness that if the world is to survive, we must not cut ourselves off physically, intellectually, or emotionally from people in other countries. This leads some people to reject out-of-hand any conception of an "American Creed" as being too nationalistic, too chauvinistic. They argue that if teachers include such a conception in their rationales, it will work against the goals of international education.

The paradox raised by such a protest is difficult to handle. The need for national cohesion, for a framework of mutual commitments from which people in our society can contend with one another, seems evident; yet so does the need for international understanding and compassion.

A starting point for dealing with this paradox is an explicit recognition that the Creed is not exclusively American, although adherence to it is an American phenomenon. The Creed's philosophical roots are many: The English culture, with its early emphasis on law and order, justice and equality; the Judeo-Christian heritage, especially its democratic notion of brotherhood in the sense that, rich or poor, we are common in the eyes of God; the European Age of Enlightenment, which sought the emancipation of human nature and highlighted the conflict between libertarianism and equalitarianism that continues to this day. And emphasis on the worth of the individual is a vital part of the culture of Native Americans (Forbes, 1973).

Commitment to the basic values in the Creed varies significantly from time to time and from country to country. The democratic tradition is more limited, for example, in Germany than in Scandinavia. And Americans seem to be more compelled than Europeans to defend their policies and actions in terms of basic ideals, wearing their values on their sleeves and constantly chastising themselves in political speeches and newspaper editorials for failing to live up to their ideals. One commentator (Myrdal, 1944, p. 4) has suggested that in contrast to other nations, "America is continuously struggling for its soul."

Despite these variations, however, the values in the Creed are clearly a Western phenomenon, not an American one. The major difference appears to be the moralistic fervor of Americans.

Is the Creed an exclusively Western phenomenon? Anthropologists May and Abraham Edel (1959, pp. 91 ff.) have suggested that concern for the worth and dignity of the individual is present in many societies and may approach the status of a universal value.

It might be tempting, but it would be a mistake to jump to the conclusion that the commitment to individual worth and dignity makes the Creed truly universal. The values in the Creed are predominantly Western in origin and orientation. Cultural differences between East and West—for example, the Chinese tendency to view time in a scope much broader than individual lives—should not be too easily discounted.

The possibility that individual dignity in the Western sense is not a truly universal value should not prevent us from judging American international behavior—our own personal actions as well as our national policy— by the values in the Creed. Moreover, if individuals made conscious attempts to identify and clarify commonalities in values across cultures, commonalities centering on human worth and dignity, they might find the common context for international debates on policy that now seems frequently to be missing. Building such a context may be the essential first step in creating a viable basis for world government.

To explore this important point, with all its ramifications (the questionable current stature of the U.S.A. as an international moral leader; potential reactions against what some countries perceive as American evangelism; the chance that cultural differences may make it impossible even to approximate a common definition of dignity), is beyond the scope of this book. We only want to emphasize that the American Creed is *not* intrinsically ethnocentric.

Certainly, an adequate rationale for dealing with values as a teacher cannot ignore the international setting of our society. Our societal commitment to human dignity should be a conscious part of the frame of reference from which teachers make decisions about international-intercultural education. And teachers should also keep in mind the potential international-intercultural impacts (for example, on the ethnocentrism of students) of value-related teaching decisions.

Democratic values, the international scene, and your teaching call for considerable thought. Value Exploration 4, p. 64, has some suggestions for reflection.

Minorities and the Creed

Another objection to the notion of an American Creed comes from the perspective of blacks and other minorities. The indictment is often stated in the form of a reproach such as "How could anyone say there is an American Creed that emphasizes values like equality and freedom, if they know how minority groups are treated in this society?"

Those who have suffered from racism can hardly be faulted for being cynical about our society's commitment to basic democratic values. Yet in their cynicism they often confuse the failure to attain an ideal with the absence of the ideal. A person who strives to be honest may not always succeed. As already noted, his lapses do not mean that he does not value honesty. By the same token, if the society or individuals in it do not always act in conformity with the basic values in the Creed, this does not mean that the Creed (that is, a commitment to the basic values) does not exist.

There can be only one (I repeat: *Only one*) aim of a revolution by Negro Americans: That is the *enforcement of the Constitution of the United States.*

—Chester Himes. *Black on Black*, 1973.

For one thing, the basic ideals of our society are lofty, and by their very nature difficult to attain. Also, we have already stressed that because the values in the Creed conflict with one another, support or promotion of one will ordinarily come at the expense of another. Extensions of freedom of speech are likely to encroach on domestic tranquility; greater equality for some—the outcome of the civil rights movement—results in limitations on the liberty of others. In no instance is any one value likely to be fully realized as the society struggles toward the ultimate ideal of dignity for all. Recognizing the conflicting nature of our basic values—which is not to deny that some people have been unjustifiably deprived of rights and opportunities taken for granted by the dominant white society—can be a powerful and valid antidote to the cynicism of youth and minorities alike.

In fact, the recent gains in rights for blacks—belated as they have been in coming—illustrate the power of the Creed. The struggle for equality has indeed been a war within America's conscience. How else can one explain the overcoming of deep-seated white prejudice except through the buffering effect of commitment to deeper values? The power of the Creed was recognized by such black leaders as Martin Luther King, Jr., who premised the nonviolent civil rights movement on the belief that if blacks could demonstrate their unequal situation and assert their demands for rights without violence, they would prick the conscience of the nation. And the peaceful sit-ins and marches and the televised confrontations with often brutal law enforcement officers did move the nation toward redressing the wrongs that blacks have suffered in this country. Policy and action were brought more in line with the commitment to equality inherent in the ideal of human dignity.

The nonviolent resister must often express his protest through noncooperation or boycotts, but he realizes that these are not ends themselves; they are merely means to awaken a sense of moral shame in the opponent.

—Martin Luther King, Jr. *Stride Toward Freedom*, 1964.

The relative emphasis placed on the various values in the Creed is continually changing. A fixed, clearly defined and ordered set of dogmas would be maladaptive in a dynamic society. Gains in equality by blacks and value shifts in other fields, such as criminal justice, prove once again that the struggle toward dignity is never-ending. Judgments about whether policies and actions take the nation in the proper direction will be largely a function of each individual's frame of reference. But the Creed, with its cognitive vagueness and emotive solidarity, does provide a viable context for confrontations over fundamental issues and for adaptation against a background of democratic commitments.

Equality of opportunity is a basic value in our society. "Get off it," says a black student. See "Equality—for Whom?", p. 65.

Recap

It is critical that each teacher in a democratic society have a clear conception of the nature of that society and of the role played by its basic values. The central position of human dignity and the basic values that define and protect dignity; the contributions of pluralism, along with the divisiveness of diversity; the importance of the emotive commitments to the American Creed; the vagueness in the descriptive meanings of the basic values in the Creed that underlies controversy, but allows change—these are all things that must be considered in developing a rationale adequate to the task of making and justifying value-related teaching decisions. Of particular importance is the recognition that the ideal of human dignity includes commitment to intelligence and to the belief that it can be improved.

Such considerations about society and the nature of values have profound implications for the school's formal and hidden curricula—for which you, as a teacher, must share responsibility. Next, we need to consider more specifically your role as a schooling agent for the society.

Mini-Democracy in Room 16

Problem *What values are at stake in the following episode?*

One of the things I've always believed is that people learn responsibility by *being* responsible—not by being *made* to do what's "good" for them. I also believe that kids can make pretty good decisions for themselves if we'll just give them a chance to do so now and then.

That's why I decided to set up a kind of democratic Forum in my sixth-grade class. My basic idea was that the Forum would be a weekly meeting—a place where we could kick around problems, make up reasonable rules for our class, and decide how to handle kids who couldn't behave responsibly. The notion, in short, was that the Forum would be "Democracy in Action," and I hoped that it would help to offset some of the authoritarian, nondemocratic modes of working that the kids were used to.

I guess the first real challenge to my mini-democracy came about two weeks after school started. The class had decided that quietness was probably pretty important during study periods, but that there wasn't any real reason to prohibit visiting *after* they'd completed their assignments. I agreed to this. I mean, it seemed to make sense at the time.

What I didn't count on was that I'd have a five-year spread in reading abilities for those sixth graders—not an unusual situation, I found out later. Some kids were finished with their work in ten or fifteen minutes, while others labored for forty minutes or more. This meant that each day the classroom talk began with low, tolerable whispering and ended up in bedlam. The situation clearly discriminated against slow readers.

I brought up the problem in our weekly Forum meeting and informed the class that I had gotten a couple of complaints from the principal. Anne Green, one of the bright, very able youngsters, challenged me right away. "I thought you said we were going to have a democracy in here," she said.

"That's right," I countered. "But we've got a problem. And I think we need to deal with it."

"You mean, *you've* got a problem," Anne retorted. "We voted on this thing. I thought we had majority rule. Either you stick by what the majority wants or we go back to the old teacher-rule thing."

I could feel the blood flush my cheeks. "What about the kids who need a little more time to get their work done?"

"Send 'em out in the hall," Anne giggled. "I say we ought to do what's good for the rest of us!"

There was applause from Anne's grinning supporters. Then it got very quiet. The kids were waiting to see what I was going to do.

Follow-up *Decide how you would probably handle this issue of majority rule versus minority rights. Find someone else in class and try role-playing the dialog between Anne and her teacher. See where it takes you in an exploration of values.*

The notion of human worth and dignity underlies both majority rule and minority rights. If students comprehend this point, it may help to resolve the conflict. Reread pages 42 to 44 for some ideas on how to handle Anne's position. (Hint: The analogy regarding a vote on genocide may make a powerful point from which you could examine the definition of democracy as majority rule.)

Devil's Advocate

Problem *Can the technique of playing "devil's advocate" be defended on the basis of developing rationality?*

The whole thing started with a series of heated discussions we had in my fourth-period class—with me playing "devil's advocate" and really forcing the students to defend their ideas about American values. Specifically, as we were talking about America's place in the world community, I was challenging the notion that America should dictate political, economic, and military policy for other countries—as we have so often in the past.

Not long after I started working in this way, there came a series of gentle inquiries, first from my cooperating teacher, then from Principal Heinlein. The principal seemed a little uptight, and I assumed that maybe there had been a complaint. But I was sure that any flack from the parents would blow over in a day or two.

I wasn't prepared for a "Letter to the Editor" that showed up in the morning edition of our community newspaper—a fairly conservative publication. It went like this:

As a parent and citizen, I believe it is my duty to inform the community that antiAmericanism is being taught at the high school. I believe America is the strongest and greatest democracy in the history of the world, and therefore feel people shouldn't always be tearing it down and criticizing it. It is getting so that any patriotism or love for our way of life is an object for ridicule. I think every person has a right to their own opinion and that a student teacher shouldn't have power over students' ideas. It is a privilege for college students to practice teaching at the high school, and I for one don't think they should be abusing their responsibility to parents. And I don't think that students who disagree with a student teacher's negative ideas should be humiliated in front of the class and have their grade lowered.

Mrs. John Umbrillo

Well, when I saw this letter, I got pretty upset. Not only was the reference to me unmistakable—since I was the only student teacher in the high school—but Mickey Umbrillo was in my fourth-period class.

I was half panicked as I tried to figure out the communication breakdown between Mickey and me. His behavior in class was always marked by a sullen kind of quietness. His contributions were brief and tight-lipped—almost *parroted*, I sometimes thought. I had only challenged him two or three times on his ideas; but I did remember how on one occasion I had staged a mini-debate in class and asked him to participate. To say that Mickey had "not done well" would be the understatement of the year. His liberal, articulate opponent had shot so many holes in his conservative position that it looked like Swiss cheese.

I didn't know what to do, so as soon as I got to school I asked my cooperating teacher for advice. She suggested that I talk with Mr. Heinlein right away to work out the next steps—the moves that would be best for the school, for Mickey and his parents, and for me. That's what I did.

Mr. Heinlein was really nice. He said that objections from parents weren't all that rare—that he got minor complaints every day, and that usually he handled them over the telephone. Sometimes, though, a problem was serious enough to deserve a parent-teacher-administrator conference. This, in his opinion, was one such problem.

"What I want you to do," he said, "is to make sure you've got a good rationale for dealing with values in the way you've been doing. In other words, I want you to explain your aims and methods in terms the Umbrillos can understand. Make it clear and to the point, okay? I'll back you up."

"I'll do my best," I said, swallowing my fear at the thought of such a conference.

"You better," Mr. Heinlein smiled. "We can't afford more letters like that last one, can we?"

Follow-up *Mr. Heinlein apparently believes that if it's good for kids to defend their values, then it's good for student teachers to defend theirs, too. Do you agree with his strategy?*

Now imagine that you're the student teacher in the conference with Mr. Heinlein and Mrs. Umbrillo. What will you say by way of rationale? Role-play this conference with two other people in class. If possible, tape-record the conversation for subsequent in-class analysis.

Chicano Maverick

Problem *Identify the three distinct value positions in the following episode.*

Jerry Burton, treasurer of the Spanish Club, was winding up the financial report. The kids were all ears. "And so, after expenses, that leaves us $88.50." Jerry grinned. "Man, we can have a real blow-out!"

Applause erupted all around me. The idea of a Spanish Club party was meeting with enthusiastic approval—and making me wince inside. I had been hoping to convince the kids that some kind of club donation for filmstrips and records might be in order, especially since our district had just gone through two years of financial belt-tightening, with no expenditures for supplemental materials.

One of the students was already at the blackboard, chalking the word "MENU" in big, bold letters. Hands were up all over the room. Janet Pritchard, the club president, glanced quickly at me. She and I had already discussed the possibility of funneling a sizeable piece of the club budget into new teaching materials.

Janet called the meeting back to a semblance of order. "Let's discuss the treasurer's report." She smiled. "We need to consider *all* the alternatives on how the club funds might be spent."

There were three or four groans from the back of the room. "A party would be fun," Janet added, "but are there any other ideas?"

As if on cue, Sharon Martin raised her hand. Sharon was just a junior and had some pretty obvious aspirations to be Spanish Club president.

"I've been thinking," she said. "I wonder if the Club might make a real long-range contribution to things around here by doing something important. I mean, why couldn't we have a party and *still* do something for the Spanish program, too? Maybe buying some filmstrips or something—I don't know. I just think maybe we could do both."

Janet gave me a small quick wink, as she thanked Sharon for her suggestion. Was there any discussion, she asked. One of the girls in the corner wondered if we couldn't split the money in half. "That's a good thought," Janet murmured. "I kind of like that idea. It means that we're doing something for our club yet still having a party. How does that sound? Do you want to take a vote?"

The response wasn't exactly enthusiastic, but I could see that things were drifting my way. The club would purchase *some* supplemental stuff for my Spanish program.

"Uh, just a minute!" came a hoarse voice from one of the corners. "I think we ought to discuss this a little bit more."

All heads turned, including mine. Miguel Garcia, an angular young Chicano student who had just recently transferred into our school, was running his fingers through his black hair. "Is this all you can think of?" he asked. "Having a party? Buying supplies for the teacher?"

His face was angry.

"Here we are, talking about this stuff, when right now there are kids in the ghettos of Mexico City going without food. How can you be so selfish? You study the Spanish language, but you don't give a damn about the people. You want to buy filmstrips? Oh, beautiful! You watch filmstrips while hungry little kids cry themselves to sleep?"

The room was utterly quiet. Janet was inspecting her fingernails while the other kids fidgeted. Finally she looked up, eying me for help.

Follow-up *Students like Miguel frequently torpedo the teacher's hidden agenda. Will you encourage maverick viewpoints even when the dissension runs counter to what you want?*
What would you do at this point in the discussion?

The Problem

Problem *Check out the implied and explicit values of the two persons in the following dialogue. Is there any point where you get the feeling that lack of shared commitments is a serious obstacle to a joint handling of "the problem"?*

"Craig, this paper is terrible. A 'D' is a gift! And you still have eight out of ten assignments left to do—and there's only two weeks left in the term. . . ."

Silence, a long silence, was the only response to my spiel, half harangue, half plea. Not even a groan or a grimace.

Nearly nonplussed, but not defeated, I went on: "We both know you have the ability. The Iowa Test scores and the I.Q. scores in your file show that. And you do get good grades in *some* of your classes. . . ."

Again, silence, not hostile, no turning away or shrugging of the shoulders. Head high, sitting relaxed, Craig was more indifferent, even contemplative.

"Hey, look," he finally said. "You know there *is* a lot more to life than getting assignments done to get marks on a report card. I mean, like getting it together. Doing things that mean something to me, not just because some teacher says, 'Do this and you'll be a success'—whatever that means."

"But, Craig." ("Careful," I thought. "No pleading. This kid's seventeen, too old for that.") "Everyone needs goals, something in life to strive for. You know . . . getting ahead, being someone. An ideal of success that helps you over the rough spots. All classes, all assignments can't be pleasant. You can't always be 'turned on.' Life just isn't that way."

"Yeah, sure, not to you. You're like my parents. Be someone! Be something! What? Who the hell am I supposed to be, anyhow? How can I be anything but me? Listen, I'm not going to waste my days getting ready for what *might* happen. I'm doing it *now,* man. Finding out, and I don't mean in books and in screwed-up, make-work assignments."

"Look, Craig, we've got a problem. And we've got to decide how to handle it. Right?"

"Yeah, man." The words sounded right but the face, friendly but disinterested, told me that *I* had the problem. Frustration! Hopelessness! How to get through?

"Craig, can we work out a schedule for handing in the assignments? Maybe if you worked here after school . . . ?"

"Well, man, I'm pretty busy. . . ."

Follow-up *What should this teacher say next? Do the teacher and Craig agree about the nature of "the problem"? About its importance? What do you think the odds are that they'll agree on how to handle it (as opposed to the teacher trying to force a solution)?*

Value Exploration 4

The section of this chapter that deals with the Creed and "The International Scene" may be subjected to various criticisms. One group of people may ask why we included the section at all. To them it will not seem relevant to a chapter on "The Democratic Context" for values education. Another group will object because the section is so brief. They will argue that in this day and age, all schooling must take place within an international, intercultural context, and that questions about the international implications of the Creed should not be passed over so lightly. Others may say it is presumptuous even to suggest that teachers ought to be concerned with engaging the "world community" in considering whether human worth and dignity is a universal value that could serve as the basis for debate. And to some, it may be an unthinkable heresy even to imply that world government is possible.

Your position on such issues will affect how you teach both your hidden and formal curricula. Some exploration of your thinking seems in order. First, write a brief statement (two or three pages) discussing your view on the world-wide application of the basic democratic values in the American Creed. You might consider questions like: Should the American Creed apply to all people? Do other national value systems differ from the Creed? If so, how? Are Americans too ethnocentric, on the one hand, or too willing to give up national ideals under international pressures, on the other? Share your paper with others in your group. Discuss the basis for any differences and the possible impact of your ideas on the things you will do as a teacher.

Then think of teaching decisions you will have to make that have to do with American values in the international context. List several of these decisions and the value implications of each. You might want to begin by considering in this context the issues raised by "Chicano Maverick" (p. 62). The following may also help you to get started:

Decision	Value Implications
Have students write to pen pals in other countries	Sharing of values is good. May help to implant American values. May lessen commitment to American values.
Read literature from other nations	Such reading may give additional meaning to American values. It may make the students question the ways in which we've applied our values abroad.
Have students participate in mock U.N. meetings	
Use Spanish Club funds to. . . .	

Equality—For Whom?

Problem *Do you agree with the following challenge to one of our society's basic values?*

It was a warm spring afternoon, and the kids in my ninth-grade civics course were restless. We'd been having this discussion about the merits of a democratic society, but somehow things just weren't clicking. I had the distinct feeling that something more than spring fever was at work in the room.

Moving up one of the rows of outstretched legs, I started my summary. "Now, in a democratic society like ours, people believe in values such as equality of opportunity and freedom of speech. This contrasts with . . ."

I was interrupted by an explosive groan from Rebecca Taylor, one of the black students. "I've had it with that baloney," she shouted. "Democratic society? Equality of opportunity? Yeah—if you're *white*. How can you talk about people in this country believing in equality of opportunity? They do, all right—so long as things are specially equal for whites. I mean, even *you* were upset last week about those two black sisters that the court had sterilized in Mississippi! How many *white* chicks does that happen to?

"And look at the scores on achievement tests! Look at who gets to be doctors and lawyers! Look at who makes the big money! Equality of opportunity is *shit!* It's all just a lot of white propaganda to keep blacks and Chicanos dumb and happy. You just want to keep us contented with what we hope we're gonna get! Whites don't *really* believe in equality of opportunity, and I'm sick of hearing about the great values of our democratic society. . . ."

Follow-up *Put yourself in this teacher's place. What do you say next? Can you build a questioning strategy based on the ideas about values and value conflict discussed in this chapter? Try it out on a colleague who is role-playing Rebecca Taylor. Then reverse roles.*

Schooling, Professionals, and Values

One purpose for our discussion of values and the nature of democracy has been to illustrate the notions of frame of reference and rationale. We also hope that being exposed to some of the results of an attempt to build a rationale for dealing with values as a teacher in America's public schools will encourage you to engage in the same type of introspection and analysis. If you have been asking yourself questions such as "Do I agree with what Shaver and Strong are saying?" "Would other assumptions be more legitimate, empirically (i.e., in terms of the scientific data available) or functionally (i.e., in terms of providing a viable context for dealing with students in the school setting)?" then our self-exposure has served its purpose.

Two other matters related to the teacher's complex, and often baffling, relationships with parents also need to be considered. One has to do with how much responsibility for students' learning you ought to accept. The other has to do explicitly with the teacher's role vis-à-vis parents. The first we will label the distinction between education and schooling; the second, the authority-agent: professional-client paradox.

The Distinction Between Education and Schooling

In common parlance, education is often taken to be synonymous with learning. That is, when someone has an experience—such as getting caught skipping school—which we hope has "taught him or her a lesson," we often speak of it as "getting an education." Stephens (1967, p. 20) noted in his provocative analysis of the school as an institution that "education can be as broad as life itself." Perhaps it would be more appropriate to say, "Education *is* life itself," for what is life but a continuous process of reacting and adapting to experiences—learning? Clearly, much—some would argue most—of our education takes place outside of school, society's formal institution for education. Our parents, other adults, our siblings, our peers, along with the other human and nonhuman elements in our environments, serve to educate us.

I never let my schoolin' interfere with my education.

— Mark Twain

Schooling, then, takes place in a broad educational context. In fact, except in specialized skill areas such as mathematics, other people and institutions undoubtedly play a more significant educational role for most children than school does. This may be partly because formalizing education—structuring it so that it can be implemented at specified times and places and with assigned people—detracts from its naturalness, and therefore reduces its meaningfulness. This lessens the school's *opportunity* for impact.

In theory, the most important purpose of school is to give an individual some assistance in educating himself. . . .

— Neil Postman and Charles Weingartner. *Psychology Today*, 1973.

To some extent, the "denaturalization" appears to be inevitable in the organization of institutions for formal schooling. But it can be minimized. It is probably not necessary to structure opportunities for educational experiences to the extent that this is done in most American classrooms. But significant shifts to more natural learning settings will only occur if teachers' and administrators' frames of reference undergo intensive scrutiny and, in many cases, revision, and if practice is then related to these frames of reference much more consciously than is now the case.

The point here, however, is that *qualitatively*, the school's opportunity for educational impact is frequently less than that of the many other educational influences that impinge on young people. And an individual teacher's opportunity for impact in such areas as values is also not as great *quantitatively* as one might think at first, given the number of hours that youth spend in school. The secondary teacher's contact with any one student is frequently limited to forty to sixty minutes in the classroom, plus unscheduled and usually fleeting encounters in the hallway and the lunchroom. The brief amount of time a student spends in each classroom does not afford much opportunity for educational impact. (Five hours a week is not much time, especially when one remembers that the teacher's personal contact with any one student is restricted by the number of students in the class.) Areas that can be specifically defined and taught for—the skills and the factual data so commonly the focus of classroom instruction—are most likely to be affected.

. . . [O]ne must make a distinction between education and school. Simply, education is a lifelong process of learning how to negotiate with the world. For "negotiate with," read: understand, accept, cope with, manipulate, triumph over, enjoy, be-one-with, or whatever is your fancy. The important part is that it is lifelong—it begins before you enter school, and ends when you do.

—Neil Postman and Charles Weingartner. *Psychology Today*, 1973.

For the institution the picture is somewhat different, because of a potential accumulative effect. Students are engulfed in the physical and social settings of the school for several hours a day each week, for several months each year. What they learn through this extended, intensive interaction with the institution and the teachers, counselors, and administrators who are also intertwined in it is frequently not at all what these people intend. But they do learn—about the institution, about the faculty and staff, about interaction with other students, about schooling as an activity.

In short, the hidden curriculum—that is, the pervasive approach to discipline, the approaches to "teaching" that are shared from one classroom to the next, the techniques of hallway-lunchroom-playground management —has a powerful educative influence. And school people ought to deal explicitly with the underlying assumptions.

Several related points bear emphasis, then: (1) Schooling is only one educational influence on youth. (2) The school as an institution may have considerable impact on students' values, but (3) the impact is often not congruent with the written or openly admitted educational objectives of the school. Although (4) the individual teacher has responsibility as part of the overall institution, (5) the opportunity for impact on values in formal classroom instruction *may* be less than he or she, or the general public, thinks.

You will need to consider all these points in building your own rationale for dealing with values as a teacher. Most laymen, when asked what they expect from the schools, probably think in terms of formal classroom instruction. Educators cannot afford to be so restrictive in their views. Whether you are dealing with parents' expectations or with your own professional expectations concerning what teachers *ought* to do about values and what they can *reasonably* expect to do, it is critical that you distinguish between schooling and education. As Postman and Weingartner (1973, 80) pointed out recently:

> . . . Thus, "to be schooled" is not the same thing as "to be educated."
>
> This view should not be construed as either an apology for or an attack on schools. . . . By pointing out the limitations of an institution, we do away with the need to defend it against unreasonable demands, and we clear the way for a realistic appraisal of what it *can* do—and might do better.

One caution, however: The distinction between education and schooling should not be used to rationalize a cop-out. It would be all too easy to say, How can they expect *us* to accomplish *anything*? Instead, the distinction should be used as one basis for setting reasonable expectations, given the many powerful educational influences that operate on students.

In short, as you develop your rationale for dealing with values as a teacher, consider carefully the distinction between education and schooling. It carries important implications for what you *should* do about values because it suggests what you reasonably *can* expect to do. You should also consider carefully your obligations and responsibilities—as an agent of the society which employs you, and as a member of a profession.

How does the distinction between education and schooling apply to specific value-related teaching decisions. Value Exploration 5, p. 79, will help you to decide.

The Authority-Agent: Professional-Client Paradox

It will help if you have a clear conceptualization of your role as a teacher, firmly grounded in a democratic frame and clarified to the point that you can communicate it, when you move, either consciously or unconsciously, into the sensitive and potentially volatile area of values. As we noted earlier, you cannot avoid treating values as part of either the formal or the hidden curriculum. Later, we will argue that for a teacher not to deal with values explicitly is, in fact, a dereliction of duty.

This position raises the very serious question: How do you, as teacher, react and relate to parents' queries, and demands, in regard to what you teach children? Your role vis-à-vis the parents of your students can be particularly perplexing because as a teacher you are, in fact, caught between two potentially paradoxical roles. You are both an agent and a professional. Thus you must view parents as both authorities and clients.

At the beginning of Chapter 3 we alluded to the teacher as an agent of society, and remarked on the complex and far-reaching implications of that role. An agent is a person empowered to act for someone else. In this sense, school people—teachers, administrators, counselors, and others— have been given the authority to carry out certain educational functions for the society. Each teacher represents the society in the classroom and during other school interactions. That is one reason why we discussed democracy so extensively in Chapter 3.

It may seem obvious that teachers function as societal agents. It is not always so obvious which educational duties they are to carry out. Nor are the processes always clear by which the society makes and communicates decisions about which functions to assign to its schooling agents.

School boards are one legitimate mechanism in the process. State legislatures are another (for example, every state [Bolster, 1962] has a law requiring the schools to teach United States history). So are state boards of education and departments of public instruction.

But how about citizen pressure groups? Or even more telling for the individual teacher, how about vocal parents who individually or in groups tend to exert their influence directly on the teacher rather than on the formal decision makers—school boards and legislatures? What should the impact of citizens, individually or collectively, be on your instructional decisions, especially your decisions about values? To whom must you or should you be responsive? Questions such as these open a Pandora's box. Perhaps they are more suitably handled in detail in treatises on school administration and public relations, but they are nonetheless critical for individual teachers.

Professional versus Agent?

Such questions become even harder to answer when the teacher's role as societal agent is juxtaposed with his or her role as professional. An agent acts for others, responding to their demands, and always striving to serve their best interests as they define them. A professional brings to his or her relationships with clients expertise in a specialized area, presumably backed by special knowledge and experience. A professional also operates within a frame of ethics shaped and policed by members of the profession. The professional frequently interacts with and does things to the client: The doctor treats his patient, the lawyer assists in setting up a corporation.

Often the professional acts like an agent. For example, the attorney expresses his client's wishes in negotiating a contract or instituting court action. While agents are typically expected to act within the common moral expectations of the society (the authority-agent relationship is no excuse for illegal behavior), society's demand on the professional is greater. He or she is expected to conform to a professional ethic. Doctors are not to prescribe medicine just because their patients ask them to. An attorney would be professionally proper in refusing to file a suit if he thought it had no other purpose than harassment.

Of course, all professionals do not live up to the ethical standards of their profession, just as they are not all equally competent in specialized knowledge and behavior. On the other hand, professionals may argue that their professional ethics supersede common moral or legal restrictions. Some medical doctors have carried out euthanasia on what they believed to be professional grounds. Attorneys have felt justified in provoking contempt-of-court charges while defending their clients.

One common, workable distinction between "agent" and "professional," then, is that the agent relationship involves one acting for another, and the professional relationship involves one interacting for and with another in a context broader than that of the other's self-interest—even, according to some professionals, broader than the common community moral standards and the laws of the society.

Now, what is the point of all this? Remember that we are discussing what you should do about values as a teacher. An important element in the frame of reference from which you make such decisions will be your beliefs about the source of your authority. Will you see yourself exclusively as an agent, hired by the local school board, and responsible only to it? Or will you consider yourself responsible to the broader society and to a conception of democracy which goes beyond local views and constraints?

These questions might also be rephrased: Will you feel obligated to follow expressed or implied local self-interests in the context of a limited authority-agent relationship? Or will you feel obligated to respond as a professional, bringing to the situation specialized knowledge and a set of professional ethics from which to approach and defend your decisions about values in the school?

These questions are not just matters for idle speculation. Although it is common to talk about the "teaching profession," we often act as if we were only agents. Teachers are often not sure what it means to be a professional—or even whether they are professionals.

A scribbled note in the mailbox. A hurried meeting with the principal just before school starts.

See "Inner Office Conference," p. 80, to zero in on the professional/ agent paradox—a dilemma in values.

Education, Law, and Medicine

One way to clarify your thinking about teaching as a profession and you as a professional is to contrast teaching with other professions, such as law and medicine. Such comparisons are fraught with latent difficulties because the teaching and the legal and medical professions do differ in striking ways. But if one approaches the comparisons by paying careful attention to differences in circumstances as well as in professional goals and roles, rather than by trying to suggest that the analogies are perfect, the process can be instructive. Let's look at some differences. Keep in mind that our concern is what to do about values as a teacher.

BE PROFESSIONAL
JOIN THE
TEACHERS ASSOCIATION!
TEACHERS ARE "PROS"
LIKE DOCTORS,
LAWYERS, AND FOOT-
BALL PLAYERS.
THEY JUST MAKE
LESS MONEY

— Sign from cartoon by Don Allen and Halsey Taylor. *Media and Methods*, 1972.

It is significant that teachers, unlike what is usually the case for lawyers and doctors, are hired directly by a governmental agency, and receive fixed salaries rather than fees based on services. You may want to explore the potential implications of this situation. Does it lead to a "stay out of trouble with the public" approach to one's work, as contrasted with a set that you must perform so well that new clients will seek you out? Do the two situations provide different opportunities for independence? If so, do these affect the willingness of teachers to take strong professional stands, even when they go counter to local public opinion? These are relevant concerns for values education.

Another important difference, one familiar to any teacher, is the aura of mystique that surrounds medicine and law—but not the teaching profession. This may be in part because of the technical language that doctors and attorneys use—derisively called "jargon" when used by educators. But there are other reasons. There *are* differences in length and intensity of training. Perhaps more important, people are not compelled to spend their childhood in daily contact with doctors and lawyers. Doctors and lawyers typically see their clients only at times of crisis. The forced and sustained contact with teachers can breed contempt at worst, and at the very least make people so familiar with what goes on in school, that each person becomes a self-styled educational expert—something that rarely happens in medicine and law.

In addition, the costs of medical and legal services fall largely on the individual client. With "free" public education, individuals are not billed directly. (Note that when voters become conscious of education costs in local bond elections, many bond issues are defeated.) In our culture, we tend to judge worth in terms of monetary cost: "If you paid for it, it must be worth it." While doctors and attorneys may often make more money because their services are worth more to the public, it is hard to avoid the conclusion that they often have more prestige simply *because* they make more money.

What does all of this have to do with values and a rationale for teaching? Because your field lacks mystique and prestige, it is especially important for you to develop a clear rationale from which to make teaching decisions. This will not only help to insure that your decisions will be sound and defensible, but it will build the type of professional relationship that allows you greater freedom of judgment, because your clients will be convinced of your expertise.

The antithesis of professional responsibility is mindlessness. Professional workers can and should be held responsible for being able to demonstrate some rational basis for whatever they do, be it research, logical thought, experience, consistency with theory or whatever.

—Arthur W. Combs. *Educational Researcher*, 1973.

A couple of other distinctions are particularly relevant to the teacher's concern with values. One is the distinction between dealing with illness and with normal growth. Both doctors and lawyers tend to deal with pathology. People commonly go to doctors when they are sick, to lawyers when they are in trouble or anticipate problems. Analogies, especially medical analogies, to the teaching profession are pernicious when they lead teachers to see their role as making students "well," rather than as participating in a process of normal, healthy development. In the area of values, for example, the former view might lead the teacher to seek out what is "wrong" with the students' commitments, rather than to help them build and clarify their own frames as part of a natural process of development and refinement.

A related difference has to do with what might be called guiding ideals. As professionals, doctors and lawyers are to guide their day-by-day activities by overriding commitments. The doctor is supposed to be committed to the preservation of life and the alleviation of suffering; the attorney, to the basic ideal of justice.

The attorney's ideal of justice is *one* basic element *in* the American

Creed. However, the medical ideals of life and alleviation of suffering are not just imbedded in, they actually transcend, the democratic ethos of human worth and dignity that underlies the American Creed and its basic democratic values. Without life and reasonable freedom from the ravages of illness, human dignity is a meaningless concept. The ideals of both professions provide fairly clear prescriptions for ethical behavior, even if the professionals are not always clear about their meanings. (The education of doctors and lawyers, like that of teachers, has little in it to help them develop rationales for professional behavior.) Of course, the ideals are not always followed in the face of conflicting demands, even when their meaning is clear.

Unlike lawyers and doctors, the teacher has no one guiding ideal, except the vague ideal of human worth and dignity, by which to set a professionally ethical course. The school's concern is with the broad spectrum of life in a democracy, not with one sector (e.g., the medical or legal elements). For that reason, the ideals that provide the teacher's professional guidance must be as comprehensive as the society itself. And it is essential to consider the nature of a democratic society when one is developing a rationale for dealing with values as a teacher.

This is a basic point of intersection between the notions of the teacher as agent and the teacher as professional. To fulfill his or her professional role, the teacher must clearly understand the nature of the democratic society to which he or she is responsible. This understanding forms the basis of an ethic for deciding when to rise above the demands of local interests. And given the concept of the professional as one who interacts with clients rather than just responding to their wishes, the teacher has an obligation to help shape the expectations of his or her clients—that is, the students' parents—to help insure that schooling does take place in a context of democratic commitment. Being able to show some special insights into the nature of a democratic society and its implications for schooling is one way to convince parents that you as a teacher bring special professional competencies to your position.

Implications for Teaching and Values

Your position as an agent and as a professional in a democratic society has direct implications for what you ought to do about values. For example, because teachers in public schools are clearly employed by the society to perform educational functions for it, it is to be assumed that they are committed to the basic democratic ethos—the basic values—of that society. A person who accepts a teaching position without that commitment has signed a contract under false pretenses—surely a sufficient reason for dismissal.

The school is not a legitimate place for subversion in the sense of encouraging or advocating the destruction of the values and basic governmental forms set up—with all their theoretical and practical limitations—to protect our evolving conception of human dignity. For example, violence is occasionally a justifiable alternative even in a democratic society, and dilemmas regarding its use are therefore a viable and fit subject for classroom discussion. In fact, what impact do teachers have on students by ignoring the existence of violence? That some people value it as an end? That others view it as a legitimate means of protecting or furthering values? To inner city students who live with violence, and to all students who experience it through the mass media, teachers who ignore violence provide further evidence that the school is out of contact with "reality."

But to *advocate* violence as a solution to problems threatens the stability of the society and runs counter to the basic commitment to a peaceful consent process. To do so in the classroom lies outside the proper role of a public school teacher responsible to a democratic society. Such action constitutes grounds for dismissal.

The classroom is not the appropriate place to advocate other political positions either. Some may protest that this stricture violates the teacher's freedom of speech, that it is the teacher's right as a citizen to express his or her views in the classroom. But that value is not involved here. The argument is not that a person should lose any of his or her rights as a citizen by becoming a teacher, but that teachers are not hired to carry out partisan political indoctrination.[1] They must function in the context of professionals for a pluralistic society with many different subgroups, none of which has a right to dominate the schools with its interests and beliefs. The teacher has no right to use the classroom as a platform for expounding his or her own political beliefs.

This does not mean that you should not express your own beliefs in the classroom or during out-of-class discussions with students. Students too often feel, legitimately, that the school and its staff are plastic, insulated and isolated from the real world as the students see and feel it. This feeling that the school and its professional personnel are artificial—along with other factors already discussed, such as the limited amount of time any one teacher spends in contact with a student—are among the reasons why teachers often have little influence on their students.

To be authentic as a teacher, you will need to express beliefs, especially when students seek your opinion. But this expression should be an educational act in the context of the values of a democratic society, not an

---

[1] Teachers should not be restricted by school boards, or anyone else, from participating actively in politics and stating their views as citizens—in fact, they should be encouraged to do so. One difficulty in teaching democratic values that have to do with commitment and involvement is that teachers frequently abstain from active political involvement. Teachers tell students that they should become active, involved citizens as adults (How about active involvement *now* in the political system of the school?), but all too often are not involved themselves, except in "safe" civic clubs such as the Lions or Kiwanis. Consequently, the students see teachers as hypocrites and gather further evidence that the school is an "unreal" place. For some excellent proposals for engaging students in the study of the school as a political system, see Gillespie and Patrick (1974).

act of political indoctrination. In this sense, the difference between the sustained and impassioned pressure of advocacy and the occasional, nonpolemic expression of one's opinion is critical.

"They *aren't* dumb," Carrie blurted out. "They're just as good as anybody! Maybe smarter! Lots of Negroes go to college and. . . ."

"Dumb jungle-bunnies," Joey interrupted.

See "Brotherhood," p. 77, to sort out your responsibilities in a tense, value-laden discussion.

Back to Subversion The connection between subversion and the expression of one's political beliefs may seem remote. Yet the previous discussion of the nature of values, and of the conflicting interpretations of values in a pluralistic society, should make it evident that, in our society, there is not likely to be consensus on what is subversive—that is, corrupting. Moreover, parents tend to overestimate the teacher's power to influence their children's beliefs and feelings. So instruction that touches on values is particularly likely to generate heat. As a matter of fact, some parents will consider such instruction subversive—even when your teaching activities are legitimate. And they may well be correct—in the sense that you will be helping students to think for themselves, and as a result they may reject their parents' value definitions and priorities.

Parents often fail to distinguish between what is subversive in their eyes and what is subversive to a democratic society. The problem is compounded when parents (and teachers) confuse the parents' role as clients with their role as members of the authority-granting society. Parents who object to what is, or appears to be, happening to their children are not likely to consider first the nature of a democratic society and the school's function in such a society. Nor are they likely to recognize that demands based on their own personal interests and biases may not be compatible with the demands of the teacher's professional role. So it is critical that you as a teacher have a clear conception of the nature of values and the nature of democratic commitments, and that you recognize your professional obligations. It is also critical that you be able to explain those obligations to parents—in the form of a rationale that emphasizes value considerations in a democratic society.

Look again at "Inner Office Conference," p. 80. How should Miss Dunning respond to a parent or to a land developer who visits her after school to object to her students' land use activities?

Recap—And Beyond

The argument in this chapter is, then, that the teacher must be responsible to a conception of democracy—as attorneys are responsible to an ideal of justice, and doctors are to the preservation of life—and that this conception of democracy must supersede strident local interests and prejudices. The teacher is not the voters' servant or the servant of the pupils' parents. He or she is an agent of the society. But beyond that, each teacher should see himself or herself as a professional with an obligation to promote education in the broad democratic context, not just to reflect the parents' or the voters' wishes.

One curious point should be mentioned here. We have argued that a teacher has no right to use the classroom for partisan politics. Yet each teacher does have an obligation to the basic values of society. Therefore the teacher must be willing to deal in the classroom with flagrant denials of these values in the local community. For example, to ignore the plight of racial or religious minorities in some communities would often be to deny one's professional commitment to an ethic based on democratic ideals.

It takes courage to deal openly with local situations that run counter to basic democratic values. Taking a stand on such issues can be not only uncomfortable, but sometimes very risky. Teachers are hired by local school boards, and local school boards are responsible, and responsive, to the local clientele—as they should be. But even professional teachers' organizations are becoming more aware that teachers have a right and an obligation to act in a context broader than that of the local community. For example, the NEA and the National Council for the Social Studies, among others, now have defense funds for teachers caught between local and professional demands.

The point is *not* that all control of the school program should be taken out of the hands of lay people and given over to professionals. It is, rather, that decisions about what the school should teach ought to be made in light of the school's role as an institution of a democratic society. By the same token, decisions about what constitutes reasonable behavior for a teacher should take into account the teacher's somewhat paradoxical responsibilities as both an agent and a professional. If you understand this point, you may be more willing as a teacher to assert yourself against unexamined local prejudices and their impact on the school. If you can communicate this point to parents, you may well make them more willing to tolerate, perhaps even to support you in your exercise of professional responsibility.

As professionals, teachers and other school people have educational responsibilities that extend beyond teaching students, and beyond adult education in the usual sense. The school cannot be expected to reform the society that supports it. But school people should help their clients—parents as well as students—clarify and develop their views of the society and of the school's role in that society.

What a blessing it would be if adults would bring to their interactions with teachers a perspective, a frame of reference, that included an understanding and an appreciation of the importance of pluralism, the inevitability of value conflict, and the implications of the democratic commitment to human dignity. That they so rarely do so is a major indictment of the schools. Next, we turn to some ways in which schooling might be made more consistent with democratic ideals, and therefore more likely to be a viable element in the student's life both during and after his time there.

Value Exploration 5

Many incidents, large and small, will arise because of your responsibility for values. In deciding what to do, you should take into account what you can reasonably expect to do. For each of the following situations, decide what the teacher's response should be. Discuss your decisions with others in your group. If you find yourself thinking about the implications of your decisions in terms of the teacher's commitment to human dignity (Chapter 3) and of the various types of values (Chapter 2), so much the better! But try to focus especially on the reasonableness of the expectation for a teacher in the schooling context.

A parent complains about her fourth-grade son's sloppy handwriting. She insists that part of the problem is that the school (and you as a teacher) have not taught him to value neatness.

Two youths are caught shoplifting. The local newspaper comments on the lack of moral education in the school.

A matron of the arts, a graduate of the local schools, condemns modern art and rock music as decadent forms of nonart that should not be allowed in the school. (Focus here on the school's responsibility for her attitudes toward esthetic values.)

A recent graduate of your high school is convicted of first degree murder. A colleague comments, "We must all share in the blame for not teaching her to value life."

A parent is disturbed that his daughter does not "value learning." He asks that you, as her teacher, try to have an impact.

Two students are having a discussion in the hallway, which you overhear. They seem confused about whether individual freedom or majority rule is more important.

Now, with others in your group, think of other such situations and discuss the appropriate responses to them.

Inner Office Conference

Problem *Identify the professional/agent paradox for Miss Dunning.*

The principal's hands were folded, his thumbs twiddling nervously. His frown deepened while Miss Dunning waited.

"Janet, you're putting me in a real spot here. The superintendent's called me twice on this thing."

"I'm sorry to hear that," Miss Dunning responded. "But my biology kids are into water sampling in a real way. If we call it off, it'll simply mean that we're capitulating to the lobbyists—the industrialists and land developers."

"But Janet—be reasonable!"

Miss Dunning smiled. "Mr. Maynard, I *am* being reasonable. Some of the factory owners and fast-buck developers have nearly *ruined* our streams. They've ignored what the wastes from their businesses are doing to our drinking water—and to our streams! It's just incredible! Why, the water-sampling project my students are doing is the first breath of *reason* this community's seen in the past twenty years! It's showing just what we're up against in terms of a community problem."

Mr. Maynard sighed elaborately. "Conducting a study is one thing," he said. "But I wonder if your students are really being *objective* about all this."

Miss Dunning shrugged. "We're gathering samples on a regular basis. We're careful in our analyses, and in how we record and summarize them. I'd call that 'being objective'."

"Now don't get me wrong, Janet," said Mr. Maynard. "I'm sure you have good intentions and all that. But aren't you inflicting your personal biases on the students? We all know you're very concerned about ecology. Isn't that your *real* motivation for doing this field work in water sampling?"

"No, I don't think so."

"The superintendent thinks you're on a muckraking campaign."

"Maybe there's a lot of muck to be raked." Miss Dunning smiled again. She chose her words with care. "But seriously, I really think the most important thing about biology is the process of inquiry. And you can't inquire in a vacuum. You have to have a problem you're trying to solve. And it just so happens we've got a beauty in this community—one that's far better than any in the lab manual, I assure you."

"I see." Mr. Maynard grimaced. "I suppose you're aware that the people you're irritating are very influential in this town?"

"I'm aware that some powerful interests would like to see us get back to our textbooks."

"And you won't reconsider?"

"No."

"Are you prepared to forego any chance of tenure in this district?"

Follow-up *The battle lines are drawn. Can the teacher's position be rationally justified? Can it be legally justified if worst comes to worst and she is denied tenure?*

How would you answer the principal's final question?

Brotherhood

Problem *Is the teacher morally obligated to express personal values in the following episode?*

The filmstrip on "Brotherhood" clicked through the last frame, and I switched on the lights. Hands went up all over my fourth-grade room.

Timmy was out of his seat. "But my Dad says niggers just cause *trouble*. He don't *want* us playin' with no black kids! He says. . . ."

"Okay, Timmy, please *sit down*," I said. "We want to have an orderly discussion."

"I think they're lazy," Lucie mumbled.

"Dumb," Joey hissed.

I glanced around my all-white class of rural kids. Carrie was jerking her hand up and down.

"They *aren't* dumb," she blurted out. "They're just as good as anybody! Maybe smarter! Lots of Negroes go to college and. . . ."

"Dumb jungle-bunnies!" Joey interrupted.

"That's about enough," I heard myself say firmly. "If we're going to have a discussion about the ideas in the filmstrip, we'll have no more of this name calling."

"But they *are* dumb," said Timmy.

"How do you know?" I asked in my calmest voice.

"*Any*body knows that," Joey grinned. "I mean, they don't even talk good, so you can understand 'em. A lotta niggers, they can't even read or write. My uncle *knows*, 'cause he's had 'em working out to his farm."

"They are *not* dumb," Carrie said. Her face was pink with emotion. "They're probably smarter than *you!*"

"Hey, nigger-lover!" Joey drawled accusingly.

"Joey, that's *it!*" I nearly shouted. "No more name calling!"
Carrie had tears at the corners of her eyes.

Follow-up *How does this discussion make you feel? What do you believe about racial differences in intelligence?*

What would you say next if you were the teacher? Look at the second paragraph of the quotation from Chester Himes' Black on Black *on p. 43. Does it provide a workable basis for continuing the discussion?*

Should you be willing to allow some students to maintain unchallenged their belief that "niggers are dumb"? If not, explore with others in your group what you might do immediately or during the rest of the school year to deal with that issue.

Teaching in a Democratic Context: Esthetic and Instrumental Values

We have spent considerable time laying out and exploring assumptions. Now we will examine some implications for your in-class and out-of-class contacts with students. The purpose is not to make prescriptions for you as a teacher, but to illustrate the importance of having an explicit rationale, set in the context of a democratic society, from which to deal with values. Of course, if some of the following ideas have an impact on your decisions and your behavior as a teacher, we will not be disappointed.

Dignity and Values in the School

Our analysis of democracy has hinged on the premise of a central commitment to human worth and dignity. It seems appropriate, therefore, assuming that students are human,[1] to ask what the ideal of dignity implies for teaching.

Do you conceive of the human as a thinking, intelligent being with a right to control his own destiny? If you take this conception seriously, you cannot see the school's proper role as only, or even primarily, the imposition of values. The school is legitimately concerned with the improvement of intelligence. And a vital aspect of this concern must be to help students

---

[1] That this seemingly facetious statement is not entirely unwarranted was confirmed by the comment of a well-meaning friend of one of the authors. When I mentioned that my two children, ages thirteen and fifteen, had enjoyed a recent skiing vacation and apparently had needed to get away from the grind of daily life for a while, the friend commented in all seriousness, "Well, I'm sure. Children are like humans." His undoubtedly unconscious slip of the tongue was significant. Too often adults in general, teachers included, forget that young people are *not like* humans, they *are* humans.

clarify their own values and, perhaps more important, learn to clarify values on their own. Helping your students to become aware of their values, to verbalize their values in terms of both cognitive and emotive meaning, to define and apply value terms, to be aware of conflicting commitments and their implications for action, and to develop the conceptual frames that will encourage and enable them to do all this for themselves out of the classroom—these goals are consistent with our society's commitment to individual worth and dignity.

This basic position—that the teacher's role is to assist each student to develop a rational foundation for his or her values, and to acquire the related analytic concepts to use after leaving school—is the fundamental theme of this book. But that theme has variations depending on the kind of values—esthetic, instrumental, or moral—under consideration.

The School and Esthetics

We have defined esthetic values as the standards people use to judge beauty. Beauty is an internal, personal experience. There is no ultimate basis for determining what should be considered beautiful, nor is there any

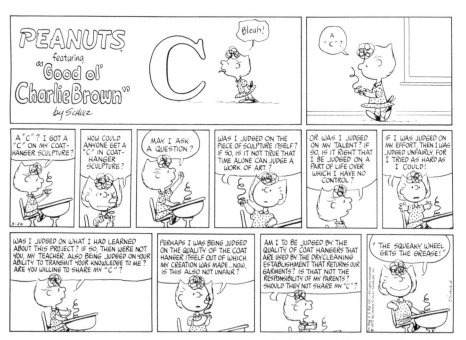

© 1972 United Feature Syndicate, Inc.

compelling reason why the society should inculcate any one set of standards for beauty. Consequently, in the context of human dignity, the school's proper role vis-à-vis esthetics is to provide opportunities—to *encourage*—but *not* to *impose*.

For the teacher of music, art, literature—or any other subject that has esthetic overtones, such as cooking—the implications are clear. One goal of such courses should be to expose students to different esthetic experiences in order to give them opportunities to expand their interests. Another goal should be to set up circumstances in which students can develop more sophisticated schemata for making esthetic judgments.

Teachers have many ways to open new vistas for their students and encourage the growth of refined esthetic standards. They can expose students to different periods of art. They can illustrate and explain composition and balance in paintings. They can play and discuss various types of music. They can have students listen to various musical instruments and discuss how the composer combines them to achieve his effects. But youngsters often do not respond the way teachers want them to, and the resulting frustration can pose a quandary: How can the teacher maintain his or her own esthetic commitments *and* a commitment to student dignity?

Part of the difficulty, of course, is that you have probably chosen to teach a subject because you are interested in it, or perhaps worst of all, because you are in love with and committed to the content. When this is the case, it can be tough to remember that the purpose of instruction is not to make the students feel and think the way you do, but to help them develop their own potentials for enjoyment and satisfaction.

In fact, there may even be a basic tension between increasing esthetic conceptual sophistication, on the one hand, and encouraging emotive sensitivity, on the other. By making students more intellectual in their approach to esthetic objects, we may detract from their ability to respond in a raw, emotional way. People, after all, can be too rational, too cerebral in their responses.

Though few of us make great or even mediocre art, the emotive, affective, feeling dimension is vital to our lives. This is why the cognitive emphasis of the curriculum in so many schools, especially in esthetic areas like music and art, makes schooling less meaningful than it might be.

Strong evidence for the general importance of the nonrational in esthetics comes from the impact of music—the art form most readily available to the majority of people. The staying power of classical music over the centuries, and the mass appeal of "popular" music—be it rock, ballad, or country-western—suggest the importance of music. Music does evoke and express poignant, feeling-centered aspects of our lives, whether we are construction workers who like to listen to the juke box in a bar after a hard day's work or faithful symphony subscribers. And, each of us gives high esthetic marks to those art forms—music, literature, or the movies—that meet our emotional needs. This is worth keeping in mind as you interact with students.

Pop music is America's most pervasive art form. It wakes us up in the morning. It rides along in our cars. It accompanies us through the bars, supermarkets, and bedrooms of our lives.

—Maureen Orth. *Newsweek*, December 24, 1973.

Our argument, then, is that a variety of "art" forms serve legitimate affective functions; we are not saying that whatever evokes emotion is esthetic. Watching someone being strangled would arouse plenty of emotion; but anyone who found it a beautiful experience could correctly be described as psychopathic.

It follows that the rational and nonrational[2] aspects of human dignity are both relevant to decisions about esthetic curricula, because emotive expression *and* reasoned judgment are both important aspects of esthetics. But because the emotional force of music—and of movies, art, and literature—meets common, down-to-earth needs, each teacher of an esthetic curriculum must weigh the potential conflict between analysis and raw, emotive experience. To strive for conceptual refinement on the part of your students should be a conscious decision, one that takes into account the possible negative, as well as positive, impacts on enjoyment if "primitive" experiencing is tempered by cognitive sophistication.

By one set of statistics, the movie business—that volatile mix of money and esthetics—would seem to have it made. A book with 20,000 readers is a best seller. A hit play may be seen by a few hundred thousand theatergoers. By contrast, 900 million tickets will be sold at movie houses across the U.S. this year.

—Paul D. Zimmerman. *Newsweek*, December 24, 1973.

There are other implications for teaching. One has to do with the subtle shifts from the esthetic to the moral that we have already emphasized (see Chapter 2). Say, for example, that you yourself prefer refined esthetic judgments. If you do not hold this preference in proper perspective, you may set a "preachy" classroom tone that clearly implies a repudiation of your students' esthetic values. Mutual alienation is likely to be the result.

Moreover, if you exclude from the classroom the very art forms that

---

[2] Note that the words *nonrational* and *irrational* are not synonyms. Because something is *not rational* does not mean that it is opposed to rationality—that it is in any sense "contrary to reason; senseless; unreasonable; absurd," definitions of "irrational" found in *Webster's New World Dictionary* (Guralnik, 1972).

the students enjoy, you may even be open to a legitimate charge of hypocrisy. After all, how can you claim to be concerned with developing your students' esthetic sensitivities when you don't, at least initially, use music, literature, or art from their daily lives as your subject matter?

The 60's are over, and nowhere is it more evident than in the world of popular music. In the astonishing creative outburst of the 60's, pop became rock and dictated the rhythms of a generation. Bob Dylan, the Beatles, the Rolling Stones and Jimi Hendrix electrified and amplified the basic black and folk roots of American popular music. Rock resurrected the blues, dealt a temporary death blow to jazz, taught country singers to plug in their gee-tars and buried Tin Pan Alley forever. To a generation turned off by war and turned on to drugs, rock was the catalyst of a whole new life style.

—Maureen Orth. *Newsweek*, December 24, 1973.

Helping students to identify and verbalize the standards that under-lie their current esthetic tastes need not prevent you from moving on to esthetic forms that you consider to be of superior quality and lasting significance.[3] What is critical is whether you accept the students' music and other esthetic forms as serious and worthwhile in their own right, or whether you show interest in them only as a stratagem to get your students interested in "really good" art.

. . . [W]hat's often forgotten is that all art is experimental at bottom. It's our tendency to equate the past with security that makes us think otherwise.

—Jack Kroll. *Newsweek*, December 24, 1973.

To develop esthetically, students will need to consider a wide range of literature, music, and art. One group of authors (Tovatt, Miller, Rice, and

---

[3] You should be careful that concern for "lasting significance" doesn't lead to the judgment that anything older is better. Adults often use this argument, for example, in disputes with young people over the relative merits of classical and popular music. It should be clear that the length of time an art work has been around does not necessarily have anything to do with an individual's reaction to it. Even though many people have reacted favorably to classical music over the years, an individual or a group of people may not find it particularly pleasurable. And how can the criterion of longevity be applied to music like that of the Beatles, which has been in existence only a few years? Beethoven was a new composer once.

De Vries, 1965, p. 2) suggests that students should be invited to bring "popular" reading material to class because:

> Expert opinion seems to agree that analysis of the "bad" as well as the "good" is important in developing reader judgment and taste. . . .

But which literature is "good" and which "bad"? Is there an implicit prejudgment of popular literature? What if you overlook the function of "popular" literature and music, and see your role as moving your students away from it (the "bad") toward the classics (the "good")? Aren't you not only likely to be seen as condescending by your students, but degrading as well?

In short, if you are narrow about esthetic judgments, if you insist that your judgments and your criteria are "right," you are denying your students' dignity. The educational impact of this denial is likely to be negative. The freedom of students to arrive at their own conceptions of what is beautiful and pleasurable—after being exposed to other forms and considering other criteria—may not be a basic value in the American Creed, but it certainly is consistent with our general commitment to human worth and dignity.

Nonesthetic Courses

If you do not teach an esthetic subject such as art or music, this discussion may seem irrelevant. But the earlier discussion of the hidden curriculum should suggest that it has important implications for you. In your formal and informal contacts with students, you make many judgments and convey many impressions. Your reaction to the paperback book a student is reading, your facial expression when rock blasts out of a transistor radio between class periods, your response when you overhear students discussing a movie they have enjoyed—each gives clear signals about your appraisal of your students' tastes.

How teachers of nonesthetic courses react to their students' esthetic judgments involves more than their abstract faith in the ideal of human worth and dignity. Whether you accept students' tastes in music and literature, whether you avoid imposing your own esthetic standards (and avoid making moral judgments based on esthetic reactions) can seriously affect your capacity to teach science or math or social studies. It will partly determine whether you can relate to your students in a way that minimizes antagonism, defensiveness, and distrust, and maximizes the opportunities for learning—by letting them know that you accept and respect their individuality.

Does math have anything to do with esthetics? "Making School Weird," page 94, raises the question whether a math teacher *should* deal with beauty.

Value Conflict

We have been emphasizing interpersonal—teacher versus student—value conflict without labeling it as such. Of course, esthetic judgments may also involve intrapersonal conflict, as when a person with broad interests in music must decide between buying a new symphony or a new rock concert recording. One of the goals of an esthetic curriculum should be to make such dilemmas more likely by broadening students' interests. Paradoxically, another goal should be to help resolve these dilemmas by making the students more aware of their own esthetic priorities.

There is another aspect to esthetic value conflict, however, that bears directly on instructional decision making. Consider, for example, two people with different esthetic tastes—John likes acid rock, Laura likes quiet baroque—who live in adjoining apartments. When John plays acid rock at peak volume, his choice conflicts with Laura's. Suppose that Laura knocks on John's door and asks him to turn down the volume. He refuses and an argument ensues. Their controversy is not likely to hinge on the relative merits of acid rock and baroque, or on the relative pleasures of low versus high sound intensity. Instead, the issue is likely to center on Laura's right to peace and quiet, to privacy in the sense of enjoying what she wants in her own apartment, and on John's right to play whatever he wants in his own apartment. In short, the argument stemming from an esthetic conflict will turn very quickly into an ethical argument revolving around moral values.

This shift is typical—perhaps we should say inevitable. But people seldom recognize that it has taken place. As teachers, we need to be aware that when interpersonal esthetic conflict leads to disputes over proper behavior, people shift from esthetic to moral values to support their positions. We can help our students to recognize such shifts and deal explicitly with the moral values involved (see Chapter 6).

Throughout this chapter we have been concerned with the potential conflict between teacher and student over esthetic values. This conflict raises the ethical issue: Can you justify imposing your esthetic preferences on your students? Your answer may depend on whether you see freedom of esthetic choice as essential to your students' worth and dignity. But freedom of esthetic choice for your students may also be an instrumental value—if you use it in order to enhance your classroom effectiveness. Of course, both moral and instrumental considerations may play a part in your decision. But it is to the handling of instrumental values that we turn next.

Instrumental Values—The Need for Dialogue

When you contemplate your role as teacher with respect to instrumental values,[4] you should also take into account the democratic society's commitment to human worth and dignity. As with esthetic values, it is important that you guard against subtle transitions from instrumental to moral judgments. That is, you must take care that your instrumental values do not become ends in themselves, and that you do not unwittingly make negative moral evaluations of students based on their failure to conform to instrumental standards (or, on the other hand, that you do not come to unwarranted positive judgments about conformers).

This is not to say that when students violate classroom and institutional rules, you should never respond with a judgment. If, for example, a youngster is constantly obstreperous or disobedient and in your opinion interferes with the learning activities of others, an ethical judgment is certainly in order. But such a judgment is different from rejecting or feeling hostile toward a student *only because* he or she does not meet an instrumental standard.

In addition, and in line with the society's central commitment to human dignity, school experiences should help the student to build a sound, rational basis for *his or her* instrumental values. Students should be encouraged to consider means-ends relationships. In a given situation, what moral end values are being sought? Do the ends justify the means? Are the instrumental values under consideration likely to lead to the desired ends? Are instrumental values taking on the tone of moral imperatives?

Self-Scrutiny

If school people are indeed committed to rationality, they themselves ought to engage in the type of critical examination suggested for students. This seems particularly important for administrators, because they influence the overall climate of a school. But individual teachers, too, should continuously ask themselves whether their instrumental standards are functional, nonfunctional, or dysfunctional—and whether they have become so committed to their instrumental standards that they are pursuing them unswervingly, as if they were ends rather than means. We believe that you ought to take time frequently to ask yourself such questions as these about

[4] Remember, these are standards set in order to achieve valued ends.

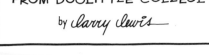

Reprinted by permission of NEA

your instrumental classroom values: Are they consistent with a commitment to dignity? Do they affront students? Are they functionally related to the learning you and your students seek?

... [W]hat is wrong with elementary and secondary education—or for that matter higher education, journalism, television, social work, and so on—has less to do with incompetence or indifference or venality than with mindlessness.

If this be so, the solution must lie in infusing the schools and the other educating institutions with purpose—more important, with thought about purpose, about the ways in which techniques, content, and organization fulfill or alter purpose

—Charles E. Silberman. *Crisis in the Classroom*, 1970.

Esthetic values are relevant here, too. Are you applying esthetic values, such as those you use to judge hair length or dress styles, as if they were instrumental values without examining the underlying, but often unexplicated, assumption that these values bear a functional relationship to learning?

Competition—a good means to an end? See "Means and Ends," p. 96.

Outcomes

Identifying and scrutinizing your own instrumental values can have several valuable outcomes. Whether done alone or in dialogue with fellow teachers, this self-examination is likely to make you more introspective and observant about the way you treat students. You may find yourself removing or relaxing unnecessary behavioral controls that arouse antagonism or impede learning. Such self-examination, then, can lead to a more reasoning and reasonable classroom, one more consistent with the notion that the ideal of dignity applies even to students.

Once you are clear in your own mind about your instrumental classroom management values, and their justification, you will be in a position to show basic respect for your students by discussing these values with them. You can emphasize their functionality as the reason for abiding by them, rather than simply insisting that students conform. The fact that you can justify these values in a way that makes rational sense to you and your students does not mean, of course, that students will never challenge them. But it does mean that such challenges can lead to rational means-ends discussions, rather than to shouted invectives, or the quiet but seething confrontations so common in schools.

If you want to explain, justify, and discuss your instrumental values, and then use them rationally in managing the learning environment, you will have to confide your goals and objectives to your students. This may seem obvious, but it is likely to be a threatening proposal to some. Moreover, you may find it necessary to go beyond the confiding of purposes and involve your students in decisions about what outcomes ought to be desired for *their* education. If students are to take part in assessing your assumptions about how your instrumental values promote learning, they must also consider the reasonableness of the learning outcomes that are sought. This, too, is a logical extension of a commitment to dignity.

Some teachers might overdo the examination of teaching purposes and instrumental values and neglect other important activities. But this is not likely, given the content orientation of most American schools. William Glasser (1969) suggests in *Schools Without Failure* that regular classroom meetings be held to work out management and other problems. Certainly a few minutes spent this way once or twice a week would not be excessive. As a minimum, a period or two should be taken at the beginning of the term to explore the goals and classroom procedures for each of your classes. Then, if regular times are not scheduled, you should at least be obviously open at any time, in or out of the classroom—to students' queries about instructional goals and instrumental values.

Although greater adherence to classroom procedures is likely to be one important result of this approach to instrumental values, the positive impact on students' feelings of self-worth and self-respect is likely to be even more valuable. If you show your students that their opinions count by involving them in decisions about the goals for their own schooling, and by having them help set the standards for the conduct of daily classroom business, their self-images are certain to be enhanced.

You must be particularly careful, though, that you do not use the process of rationalizing instrumental values simply to dupe or seduce students into conformity. Many young people are rightly wary, after years of being put down by the system. They can readily sense—and even imagine—insincerity, and they will take it as evidence that you do not respect them. You must give serious consideration to your students' opinions, without condescending to them, and without making explicit or implicit threats of retribution toward students who speak their minds. If you open the ends and means of the classroom to discussion, treating students as humans capable of thought, you must be ready to have your own conclusions challenged. This will be uncomfortable, perhaps impossible to handle, if you need to rely on an authoritarian relationship to maintain a "superior" position over your students.

Are you clear on the instructional implications of instrumental values? To check your comprehension, turn to Value Exploration 6, p. 98. It will help focus your thinking on some basic questions.

Recap

Showing respect for students' esthetic judgments and involving students in establishing instrumental values are both consistent with a commitment to human dignity. Both are also likely to make the school a more meaningful and less inimical place for the young. As the student's perception of the school changes and student-teacher relationships are transformed, the job of teaching could become much more pleasant than it often is now.

The basic question raised here is the question we raise throughout this book. How do *you* view the young? Do you really see them as capable, functioning humans, deserving of your respect? Or do you see them as juveniles upon whom the judgments of mature adults must be imposed? Does your in- and out-of-classroom behavior truly reflect respect for students? Perhaps no questions are more critical than these to the development of the rationale from which you will make your value-related decisions as a teacher.

Making School Weird

Problem *Zero in on Mr. Graham's concern for esthetic values in his seventh-grade math class of inner city kids.*

"Hey, far out! What's he got now?"

"I don't know, man. Looks *weird!*"

Butch Morgan and Tino Muella were drifting into the strangely ordered world of Mr. Graham's seventh-grade math class, a place that always seemed to quiet the chaos of city streets outside. This was the class they both looked forward to each morning, though they had been hard pressed to explain why when Mr. Graham asked them to fill out a semester course evaluation.

It wasn't that the class was easy. Emphatically *no* on that one. It wasn't even that Mr. Graham was black and hip and drove a low-slung sports car, though that counted for something. It was simply the "weirdness" of the class, as Tino liked to put it. You never knew what crazy thing he'd have you doing; and then, afterwards, he'd have you figuring out stuff you didn't know you could do on your own. Somehow, it was different from the other classes that put you mentally—and sometimes physically—to sleep.

"Hi, dudes." Mr. Graham's glance flicked up, then back to his work. "How you making it?"

"Cool." Tino shrugged and jammed both hands into his hip pockets in a gesture of studied nonchalance. "What's happenin'?"

"Monday morning," Mr. Graham said.

"So what's that thing?"

"Nothing special. Called a geodesic dome."

Tino poked his tongue in his cheek and shifted his weight. Butch grinned at him.

"Get your homework done?" Mr. Graham asked, still concentrating on his work.

"Yeah."

"Good."

In a few minutes, twenty-four kids were jammed around the work table, and Tino was showing them how to clip the polygons together. A huge dome was taking shape. Meanwhile, Mr. Graham was taking roll and filling out the absentee form. A Monday morning with no kids absent. He took pleasure in this and smiled to himself as he moved into the crowd.

"What's it for?" Juanita was asking.

"Well, it could be the building of the future," Mr. Graham said. "Both on earth and out in space. Do you see why?"

"Easy to put up," Miguel said.

"And light," Gary interrupted. "Man, you could put jillions of these little sticks on a rocket ship! Give them astronaut dudes something to do at night."

"Right on," Mr. Graham said. "Of course, this is just a model. Real buildings like this one are enormous. But you've got the idea. It's lightweight and incredibly strong for the weight of its separate pieces. And, to me, its simple lines are really kind of beautiful—you know? Tougher looking than the boxes we live in. And, of course, it's simple to put together, too—even you guys can do it, huh?"

"Hey, listen to that," Tino grinned. "We do *his* work, and he starts badmouthin' us."

Mr. Graham snickered in a friendly way and handed a triangle to Marsha so she could add it to the dome. "C'mon, now. Quit admiring the thing. You guys really think you can figure out why it's so strong for its weight?"

"Yeah," Butch grinned. "We'll figure it out. We ain't dummies, you know."

"True enough," Mr. Graham nodded. "Looks like you're *domeys* today!"

Follow-up *Part of Mr. Graham's lesson plan involves having students try to crush a raw egg by squeezing it. In this way, they will learn something about how the fragile beauty of the eggshell distributes pressure. He hopes that such experiences will pique the students' curiosity and cause them to seek mathematical explanations. Is he teaching esthetic values if he has students compare the beauty as well as the strength and "usable life space" of a geodesic dome with other geometric forms such as cubes and pyramids? Should he do so?*

The "esthetic response" often occurs when you understand something in a new way—when the strange is made familiar, or the familiar strange. Try to remember an occasion in your schooling when a teacher helped you "see" the subject matter from an exciting or profound perspective. Or try to recall a time when you "put things together" on your own—the feeling when you really understood for the first time the basics of something you were studying. Discuss the personal value of such an esthetic experience with your friends. What does it do for you when it happens?

Means and Ends

Problem *How can failure to think clearly about means affect the ends a teacher wishes to achieve?*

"T.G.I.F." Marty Donahue grins. "And *salúte!*"

There's great enthusiasm for Marty's impromptu toast around the table. Three other teachers hoist their beer mugs, echoing his gesture.

"Two days of freedom!" Gil Hunt says.

Judy Washburn, the girls' P.E. teacher, smiles and shakes her head. "Freedom? What a sick, sexist joke! Andrea and I have got a week's housecleaning to do, you muttonheads!"

"Ms. Washburn, that's *good* for your physical fitness." says Marty. "Keeps you in shape!"

"I ought to clobber you," says Judy.

"No, no," Gil frowns, "that would be out of order during our serious discussion of the week's problems."

Judy sips her beer and tries to keep from laughing. "Okay," she says. "I guess I'm really having a problem in my P.E. program right now. You see, my chart isn't working."

"Tell us more," says Gil. "Marty and I will help you sort things out."

Judy takes a deep breath and starts to outline the problem. How she's talked herself into believing that a huge locker-room chart which showed the relative skills of each girl would increase motivation and help spark her program, but how things have been going from bad to worse ever since she implemented the idea.

"To compete or not to compete," says Marty. "A real value dilemma—wouldn't you say, Gil?"

Andrea Thomas, who has been hanging back until now, comes into the discussion. "That's *exactly* what it is, you clowns. The way I see it, Judy's working through a problem in instrumental values."

Marty and Gil exchange stunned, silent looks.

"We're not following you," Gil says.

"Okay." Andrea nods. "Judy's told us that she thought competition, created by a master chart, would motivate the girls. In other words, she's used competition as an instrumental value—a way to help the girls achieve the things she wants them to in P.E."

"Right," Judy says. "And it isn't working."

"Could be because the girls with really low skills are discouraged by this kind of competition," says Andrea. "Nothing makes a kid feel crummier than a public record of low achievement."

"So competition is a bad thing?" Marty asks.

Andrea shrugs. "I guess it depends. If you've got a chance of winning you probably feel challenged by competition. But if it looks hopeless, you're probably going to feel pretty discouraged and threatened."

A smile begins to edge across Judy's face. "Maybe I could get them to compete against their own *past* performance," she says.

"Might be worth a try," says Andrea. "After all, it's not competition against each other that you're really concerned about, is it? The competition's just a means to help you achieve your goals."

"Wait a minute," Gil says. "Hold everything, I'm confused. I thought competition was the basis of Western Civilization! I thought we were trying to prepare students for *life!* Isn't competition a part of life?"

Judy is wearing the patient expression she reserves for slow learners. "Mr. Hunt, competition is indeed a part of life. But it probably isn't a *moral* value that's good in and of itself. That's just a phony bill of goods!"

"Women's Lib," Gil grunts. "Whoever heard such screwy ideas before, huh? I think we need another beer!"

Follow-up *Can competition be both an instrumental and a moral value? What do your friends who are reading this book think?*

Were you surprised when Andrea Thomas said, "Judy's working through a problem in instrumental values"? How do you think teachers who hadn't read this book would react if you said something like that during a bull session? What would you say if the reaction was "Horsefeathers!", or "What's this nonsense about instrumental values?"?

Value Exploration 6

Turn back to "Instrumental Values, Kids, and Potted Plants" on page 37. Reread it with the following questions in mind:

Is there any evidence that Mrs. Ashcroft has periodically reexamined her instrumental values of neatness, predictability, and order?

Could it be that these values have become end (moral) values in her mind?

Are her instrumental values likely to be counterproductive for some kinds of learning? What kinds?

Do you think Mrs. Ashcroft could handle (tolerate) the suggestions made in Chapter 5 for involving students in setting up and scrutinizing instrumental values?

If you were the principal of her school, would Mrs. Ashcroft's approach bother you? If so, how might you go about trying to change her outlook and behavior? If change were not possible, would you consider dismissing her?

Discuss your responses to these questions with others who have read "Instrumental Values, Kids, and Potted Plants." In particular, try to express divergent views so that the assumptions underlying the above questions will be explored. For example, despite her approach, which may seem restrictive to some, Mrs. Ashcroft may be a very loving teacher who respects and has the respect of her students—and teaches them some significant attitudes toward rules.

Teaching in a Democratic Context:
Moral Values

Moral values, as we defined them in Chapter 2, are our standards for judging whether aims or actions are proper. They are an essential basis, implicit or explicit, for our ethical decisions.

Now esthetics are important to a rounded and satisfying life, and we need to examine our instrumental values to insure that we do not fall into the trap of confusing means with ends. But esthetic arguments are preempted by ethical ones as our esthetic choices begin to impinge on other people; and our instrumental values must ultimately stand or fall on their utility in maintaining moral values. For these reasons, moral values are more fundamental and of higher priority in values education. This is true for teachers in every field, not just in social studies where the emphasis on citizenship education makes moral values particularly relevant.

Some time you may have the chance to help develop a sequential program for moral values education. More likely, however, you will find yourself dealing with moral values in bits and pieces—in short units or incidentally in the formal and informal curriculum. In any case, a rationale for dealing with moral values needs to consider the components of intelligent valuing and some of their implications for teaching. The purpose here is not to propose a program for values education. We do, however, want to relate some notions about democracy and the nature of values to teaching about moral values.

Cognitive Aspects of Moral Values Education

Our discussion of the nature of values in Chapter 2 emphasized their cognitive and affective aspects. By the same token, in our consideration of democracy, we have stressed the intellectual relevance of values (rationality as an underlying component of our commitment to human dignity and the necessity of untangling our value commitments in order to make sound decisions) and their emotional relevance (value commitments as the context for meaningful disputation and as the "cement" for a vast, multicultural society).

The following discussion begins by focusing on the cognitive. It then moves specifically to an affective topic. We deal first with cognitive aspects of valuing: Identifying and clarifying our values; the importance of value labels; dealing with the consequences of acting on our values, which includes handling value conflict; relating moral values to decisions. Next we discuss value inculcation. Here we will deal with a fundamental question raised by the affective side of values.

Identification and Clarification of Values

Our democratic commitment to rationality does not assume a purely intellectual approach to life. Our behaviors are, and should be, influenced by our emotions. But it is desirable to be aware of the forces that move us. That is, remembering that values are both cognitive and emotive, one step in the direction of rationality is to try to state what our values are. What are our standards? How strongly do we feel about them? Answering such questions we call *value identification.*

Reprinted by permission of Jules Feiffer

Statements of identified values often have no clear cognitive or emotive meaning. Emotions are hard to put into words. And trying to be aware of and convey to others the cognitive meaning of a value can be difficult because one tends to confuse feeling with intellectual meaning. In addition, values are not static—either in the society or in any one individual —so a statement that is accurate at one time may not be so at another. For all these reasons, it is important to help your students go beyond a surface identification of principles and related feelings. The point is to help them be as certain *as is possible* at any time about the parameters of their commitments. So moral values education must involve not just value identification, but *value clarification* as well.

As we have suggested, value clarification is not easy. Witness the difficulties faced by the Supreme Court in defining the basic values underlying most of its decisions. What is meant by "due process of law," for example? Has it been denied to a defendant who did not have an attorney when he was tried? What does "equal protection of the law" mean? Can it be considered to exist when laws require that students be segregated by race? How about when the segregation is *de facto* (existing in fact) rather than *de jure* (by law)? The Court has answered differently at different times—on these and other issues—as citizens have challenged current definitions or applications of values. If you are interested in obvious transitions in value meaning, study any of the series of cases that report the Court's attempts over the years to define various basic values.

Value Labels

Thinking about values, like thinking about anything, depends on language. We need to pay special attention to *value labels,* especially labels for the central moral values that we call basic values. Value identification and clarification are partly a question of defining value labels clearly. But there is more, too. Moral values education in a democratic society should teach students to use value terms that relate their unsophisticated value concepts to the more basic, more general values of the society. This we call *label generalization.*

The terms that adults as well as children use in applying their values to concrete situations often do not "fit" with the language of political-ethical debate. Take, for example, the notion of "fairness" which children and youth develop and apply in play as well as in the classroom. "It's not fair," may be said of a playground game in which, via some biased process, all of the best student athletes arrange to be on the same team. Or, "It's not fair," may be used to protest a referee who favors one team over the other. In the first instance, the idea of "fairness" is akin to the political-legal concept of equality of opportunity. In the second, it is akin to the political-legal concept of equal treatment before the law. And a youngster who protests, "I've got a right to say what I want," when an adult shushes him during an argument, is calling on a value that might appropriately be termed freedom of speech.

Helping students to begin to use labels with basic value meanings serves several related instructional and societal functions: (1) It provides a basis for value identification and clarification.[1] (2) It gives students a more powerful conceptual scheme as they relate their own untutored commitments to the basic values of the society. (3) It gives students a more powerful value language for analysis, discussion, and persuasion. And (4) it helps to insure a nationwide values vocabulary at the basic value level among people who, unlike news commentators, politicians, and lawyers, frequently would not otherwise use such terms in their thinking and disputes. In short, the process of label generalization is important because it relates the student's own developing value vocabulary and conceptual schema to the broader and more powerful basic values of a democratic society.

A news item sparks a heated discussion.

"Well, I don't think it's *fair!*" a white ninth grader blurts out.

"Fair?" comes the incredulous challenge from a black student.

Turn to "Current Events," p. 112, and consider the values clarification and identification problems involved.

Consequences and Value Conflict

Another basic element in rational valuing is the *examination of consequences.* This simply means asking: "What will happen if people do (or do not) act in accord with, or support, a particular principle?" We are not likely to be clear about the dimensions of our value commitments until we examine what may happen if we act upon (or ignore) them.

When students examine consequences, they will probably discover that acting on the basis of one moral value commonly leads the person to violate another one. Such value conflicts involve personal preferences, the middle-level values (such as honesty) that are so important to one's personal relations with others, and the basic values that are used to justify decisions about personal and societal questions of proper aims and conduct.

Value conflict recognition ought to be treated as more than an incidental outcome of examining consequences. Our values are inherently inconsistent and their relative importance changes over time. Because the

---

[1] Two questions are pertinent here: Is the value that is being applied to a personal situation similar to the value referred to by the broader value term? Is it appropriate to apply the broader value to this particular situation? The latter question is not the same as asking whether the value is being applied correctly. The distinction is between "Is John's freedom of speech really at issue here?" and "Should Mrs. Jones have denied John his freedom of speech by telling him to shush?"

potential of value conflict is so pervasive students ought to learn to recognize and deal with value dilemmas openly and rationally.

The disputes that can make value conflicts obvious may not occur in your classroom if the class is homogeneous. People with similar frames of reference are less likely to have interpersonal value conflicts on basic ethical issues, or to stimulate one another to self-examination. To bring out different points of view, you may have to take a devil's advocate position, or use student role-playing, films, or outside reading. The devices you use should awaken your students to the existence of, and reasons for, conflicting opinions in the society (see, e.g., Fraenkel, 1973, pp. 238–255).

Once value conflicts are recognized, they should be confronted and handled. This stage of valuing we call *value conflict resolution.* As Coombs and Meux (1971, pp. 54–61) have pointed out, it may involve any or all of the following: Examining similar situations to see if you would be willing to accept the consequences of acting on one or another value in each case; changing places (usually in a simulation of some sort) with a person who will be affected by the application of the value, in order to consider whether you could accept the principle if you were in that person's shoes; asking if you could accept the consequences if everyone acted on the principle in question. The examination of consequences, then, is obviously important both as a means of making value conflicts salient and as a means of arriving at an acceptable resolution.

Handling value conflict is especially important when we apply basic values to the justification of political-ethical decisions (decisions about public issues). The search for human dignity demands that we weigh conflicting basic values (such as equality and freedom), and deliberations about public issues should proceed from that perspective. In fact, as noted above, it is important to teach students to search out the basic values that support their opponent's position—or, if they are not directly involved in a dispute but are trying to make a disinterested decision, to look for the basic values on each side of the issue.

We must be willing to keep our value choices open to reexamination. We have used the phrase *value conflict resolution* for want of a better term. As we noted in Chapter 2, however, our value weightings shift, and the same value conflicts occur in settings sufficiently different that our value choices change. Value conflicts can, therefore, be resolved once and for all only by individuals who are cognitively inflexible.

Although it is seldom possible to resolve value conflicts permanently, it is important to use some consistency in applying one's values. No one wants to be in a constant state of quandary. Moreover, other people are entitled to have some reasonable expectations as to your behavior. We want to avoid the implication that shifting value emphases is "good" in itself—any more than it would be "good" to maintain a consistent value position in the face of changing circumstances. We should use our rationality to weigh our value priorities, remembering that "stability" and "adaptability" are both values to be taken into account.

Summary You will assist your students along the road to rational decision making if you can do two things: (1) Make them aware that value conflict is inevitable, so that they do not see having to confront value dilemmas as a sign of abnormality or malfunctioning. (2) Help them learn to weigh values—for example, in terms of the consequences of following conflicting commitments—and come to tentative conclusions while accepting that value dilemmas are not resolvable in any final sense. These are not impractical goals. If you succeed in achieving them, perhaps you will help to reduce dishonesty on the part of government officials, the questionable business practices so common today, and the unconscionable treatment of blacks and other minorities in this country. In short, you may help people to do better at matching what they say to what they do.

Valuing and Decisions

A decision is the desired result of the ethical reasoning process. In particular, we should help students arrive at *qualified decisions*. A qualified decision is one that takes into account the possible negative consequences of a policy or action to be supported, and the circumstances under which you might change your mind and support a different value. A qualified decision might also take into account the extent to which it depends on particular definitions of key terms, including value labels.[2]

Cheating on a quiz—time for a lecture or an opportunity for some value analysis? See "Story Within a Story," p. 113.

Judging Decisions The democratic society's commitment to human worth and to rationality suggests that all sides of an issue should be given consideration in decision making. This does *not* mean, however, that differing positions must automatically be given equal weight. Teachers can judge the complexity and soundness, and therefore the acceptability, of their students' position statements (see, e.g., Newmann and Oliver, 1970, pp. 278–284; Oliver and Shaver, 1966). And they can help young people learn to apply these criteria to their own and other persons' position statements.

For example, one can question whether the consequences of acting on a given value have been adequately examined and taken into account.

---

[2] For a discussion of qualified decisions, see Shaver and Larkins (1973a, Ch. 9).

This may involve asking whether the person considered conflicting commitments before he arrived at a position.

Value Conflict and Relativism Educators have expressed concern that our value conflict rationale might lead students to believe that because value conflicts cannot be finally resolved, decisions cannot, or need not, be made. That is, students might use their awareness of value conflict as an excuse for copping out—or for not confronting a decision, on the relativistic grounds that anyone's position is as good as anyone else's.[3]

We have already noted that positions can be judged by the adequacy of the reasoning behind them. Moreover, it should be clear that decisions do have to be made. Neither personal lives nor world affairs stand still merely because value conflicts are difficult to grapple with and resolve. This is where the qualified decision comes in. Since decisions must be made, the rational person takes into account the qualifying circumstances that condition his or her stand. In your classroom, therefore, you should emphasize that decision making is inevitable, that action is necessary, and that even inaction implies a decision—the decision not to act.

This brings us back to a question we discussed in Chapter 4. In dealing with issues that involve value conflict, should a teacher ever take a stand during classroom discussions? We suggested in the earlier discussion that your willingness to be identified with a position may go a long way toward convincing students that you are not a phony or an uncommitted person. Now we want to add a second point: If you refuse to let students know where you stand on issues, your refusal may be interpreted as relativistic. Such a stance certainly does not provide a model of involvement in decision making appropriate to a democratic society.

Our recommendation that you be willing at times to let your students know what you believe is not likely to cause much consternation when you are dealing with historical issues. For example, no one is likely to be too upset if you express moral revulsion at the Nazis' "final solution" to the "Jewish problem," toward the institution of slavery, or toward the treatment of Indians in the nineteenth century.

But what about issues of current, even local, concern? Is it realistic to ask you to take a stand on matters that may frighten or enrage parents (and, consequently, administrators)—especially when to do so may cost you your job?

Here the value conflict model is again relevant, because it provides you with the means of taking a stand. The model provides a framework of rationality for teaching students to deal with issues, and therefore, a basis for stating your position. Using the qualified decision, you can take a stand

---

[3] If the relativistic argument interests you, you may wish to read an argument by Oliver and Shaver (1974, p. 50) that relativism is an inappropriate and nonfunctional basis for curriculum development and teaching in a democratic society.

which does not attack those who disagree with you, but rather takes into account their deep concerns. Note, however, that the statement of qualified decisions is likely to temper your students' emotional responses only to the extent that they understand value conflict and are accustomed to taking contradictory values into account in their own decision making.

In other words, when students have been helped to develop an adequate frame for analyzing controversial issues (see, e.g., Shaver & Larkins, 1973a), your statement of opinion in the classroom is potentially less "dangerous." Students are less likely to take it as an attempt to impose your views on them or as a pronouncement to be accepted unthinkingly.

We make the following statement from experience: When you and your students share an analytic frame, and when, in addition, you conduct discussions in a context of dignity, clearly based on the assumption that your students are intelligent, worthwhile beings whose thoughts and comments are to be respected, your position simply becomes one among others to be considered. You can let students know that you stand for something—and do so in a rational setting that makes clear that you do not intend to indoctrinate them.

Your students ask you to take a stand. How might you respond? Value Exploration 7, p. 115, asks you to deal with that question.

The mention of indoctrination leads us to our next important point.

Affective Aspects of Moral Values Education: Inculcation and Dignity

Decisions about moral values education based on a commitment to human dignity must be concerned with cognitive outcomes; but there are also important affective considerations beyond the emotions that might be raised by discussions of value-related issues. These become apparent when we raise the basic question: Should teachers in a democracy indoctrinate values? Or, put another way, Should your role as a teacher include value inculcation, especially when this involves instilling deep emotional commitments to certain values?

We have already made our position clear in regard to esthetic and instrumental values. In the area of esthetics, the teacher should not indoctrinate. Rather, he or she should try to help students develop their own sets of criteria for beauty. In fact, attempts to implant values in areas such as music and English often misfire. Pious comments about the students' failure to appreciate the "right" kinds of music or literature often only confirm the image that many young people have of teachers as, at worst, inconsiderate and disrespectful, and at best, well-intentioned, but rather bumbling souls out of contact with reality.

By the same token, the teacher should not inculcate the instrumental values of the school. If you respect your students, you must explicate and examine with them your justifications for instrumental values—that is, how you expect these values to help obtain the end results you want. And you must alter or discard those values when they appear to be nonfunctional or dysfunctional. And, of course, instrumental values which lead to violations of dignity ought to be abandoned, regardless of the ends they achieve. Inhumane methods are not to be justified on the basis of valued ends.

Moral values call for a different initial approach, but the end result in terms of teaching behavior is similar. To begin with, recall the earlier discussion (Chapter 3) about the fundamental function of the American Creed. Not only do the values in it provide a linguistic and emotive frame for political debate among the diverse groups in our pluralistic society, but as a corollary they provide the cohesive force (the "cement") that holds divergent groups together as a political entity.

Teachers, as professionals in a democratic society, therefore have special obligations in regard to these values—as distinct from personal preferences and even middle-level values. Teachers have no business attempting to impose lesser values. But they are obligated to encourage emotive commitment to the basic values of the society, as well as growth in the cognitive processes of value identification, value clarification, and value conflict resolution.

In colonial America, freedom of the press could not be taken for granted. John Peter Zenger, a German immigrant and editor of the *New York Weekly Journal*, was imprisoned for criticizing the governor of New York. In 1735, after ten months in jail, he came to trial on libel charges. To the British court, the only question was whether Zenger had published critical articles. His attorney, Alexander Hamilton, argued that he should be convicted only if what he said was untrue. The jury agreed with Hamilton and the foundation was laid for freedom of the press in this country.

Emotive commitments tend to be formed at an early age—studies of political attitudes (Massialas, 1969) suggest before and during elementary school. Literature and other materials (such as dramatization of the John Peter Zenger free press episode) can be used to build commitment to basic values by exemplifying their importance and the dedication to them in our society. Such experiences should be an important part of elementary school teaching (see, e.g., Oliver, 1960). But for teachers at all age levels the teaching role is more likely to be the *reinforcement* of often unverbalized value commitments, rather than the instilling of new values. That is, you may be able to make existing commitments stronger, but the commitments themselves will usually have been established in the powerful environment of family and peer groups, and via television.

In a very important sense, then, the issue of value inculcation or indoctrination by teachers is a red herring, because forces other than the school are relatively more powerful. Unfortunately, this issue is still so emotionally loaded that it often prevents us from exploring the teaching behaviors that are legitimate in a democratic educational context.

Value inculcation is a red herring in another sense—if one agrees with our discussion of values, especially the emphasis on the affective and cognitive aspects and functions of values, in Chapters 2 and 3. It should be obvious that *the legitimate inculcation* (or more realistically, the reinforcement or strengthening) *of commitment to basic democratic values does not entail indoctrination of any particular cognitive definition of the values or any particular political position.* How the values are to be defined and which opposing values are to be given preference must be left for students to decide themselves. If you as a teacher emphasize, for example, values having to do with freedom—and neglect the opposing values of equality and security (or vice versa)—you are violating your students' human dignity.

Here the distinction between values and value judgments (see Chapter 2) is crucial. *It is justifiable to build emotive commitment to the values basic to a democratic society. It is not justifiable to indoctrinate specific judgments based on those values.* You would be out of line, for example, in trying to convince your students that welfare was bad policy[4] because it deprived people of their independence—or, on the other hand, that it was good policy because it made people more equal.

An organized sitdown strike: What are the implications for value inculcation? This question is posed by "Pep Assembly," page 115.

How about Parents? You may be asking yourself, But what about my students' parents? Won't they be upset by my attempts to indoctrinate or consolidate emotive commitments to *any* values? These questions recall the discussion of the teacher as professional in Chapter 4. They should remind

---

[4] Note that we have used the word *policy* instead of *value judgment*. Policy is a broader word. A value judgment is an assertion based on a value; policy is a plan or course of action. A typical policy may be thought of as a complex judgment based on a value (or values), but also on factual assumptions that may themselves be very complex.

you that it is important to have a carefully thought-out rationale for making teaching decisions, and for discussing these decisions with fellow teachers, administrators, and parents.

Parents may find it harder to tolerate rational valuing than inculcation. They are likely to think that teaching is subversive when it leads youngsters to challenge the unexamined value assumptions of the home. This is another reason why you should be circumspect about translating value commitments into value judgments.

Parents would be particularly likely to tolerate inculcation of certain middle-level values, such as honesty, punctuality, and dependability, because they want youngsters to exhibit these daily in their interactions. They may not, for example, be particularly happy if, rather than insisting that "Honesty is good," you ask such questions as:

"What is meant by honesty?"
"What may be some consequences of not being honest?"
"Under what circumstances (that is, when confronted with the violation of what other values) could one justifiably choose not to be honest?"

Such a pattern of questioning is essential, however, if you are to help students build rational bases for their value stands.

As a professional educator in a democratic society, shouldn't you be prepared to argue not only that parents should tolerate such inquiry, but that they should encourage it as a legitimate and needed educational function of the school? Certainly, this task is not likely to be carried out systematically elsewhere. One seldom overhears this kind of dialogue at parties or in more intimate discussions among friends. The home itself, where so much education takes place, is a difficult environment for critical inquiry into values. The relationships there are too complex, too fraught with emotive power. Moreover, it is too difficult for parents, in their intense relationships with their children, to stand outside their own frames of reference, to be analytic, and to ask questions in ways that are not overt or subtle reminders (deliberate or not) of what the child *ought* to believe, rather than invitations to contemplation.

Moreover, the concept of human dignity, emphasizing individual choice and rooted in the notion of pluralism, demands that, important as the home may be, a broader context for value development is necessary—for the good of the maturing individual as well as in the interests of the society. Kahlil Gibran (1923) has expressed, as only a poet could, what human dignity means in child rearing. With slight modifications, his words are also a poignant reminder to teachers who would impose their own value interpretations and choices on their students:

Your children are not your children.
They are the sons and daughters of life's longing for itself.
They come through you but not from you,
And though they are with you yet they belong not to you.
You may give them your love but not your thoughts,
For they have their own thoughts.
You may house their bodies but not their souls,
For their souls dwell in the house of tomorrow, which you cannot visit, not even in your dreams.
You may strive to be like them, but seek not to make them like you.
For life goes not backward nor tarries with yesterday.
You are the bows from which your children as living arrows are sent forth.

. . .

Let your bending in the archer's hand be for gladness. . . .

You may want to explore with some of your fellow teachers the implications of Gibran's words for your interrelations with parents and with students. How many parents or teachers can accept such an expression of dignity for youngsters? Do we unjustifiably deny the worth of the young by trying to mold them in our own images rather than "shooting forth the arrow"? Does Gibran's statement have any relevance to the frequent alienation between parent and child, or between school and student?

About teaching itself, Gibran says:

If he [the teacher] is indeed wise he does not bid you enter the house of his wisdom, but leads you to the threshold of your own mind.

Recap—And Beyond

Each of the various components of valuing—values identification and clarification, label generalization, examination of consequences, value conflict and resolution, and commitment—needs to be considered in making teaching decisions. The components are not valued ends themselves. They take on importance in light of the democratic commitment to human dignity, and therefore to intelligent decision making. Each of these components of valuing is significant to the extent that it helps individuals to make sound decisions in the ethical domain by increasing the probability that these decisions will be consciously related to their commitments.

The cognitive aspects of moral values education discussed in this chapter are not intended as an exclusive definition of rational moral valuing. We think that these components are significant; but we present them here as suggestive and heuristic, not as definitive, final answers. Consider them as you contemplate what to do about values. But remember, they can be refined and expanded.

Note, too, that the discussion in this chapter is focused on operations for clarifying and dealing with values. We have almost totally ignored other aspects of intelligent decision making. For example, we only touched on the problem of handling factual questions in making decisions—by suggesting that people should examine potential consequences when making value choices. Another important area, language clarification, is hinted at in the discussion of label generalization. Many other concepts and skills are needed to handle factual and language problems in making warranted, sound decisions. But to discuss them all is beyond the scope of this book.[5]

Another caveat: The order in which we have discussed the aspects of a values education program is not necessarily the order in which you ought to teach them. That is, in teaching about values, you will not necessarily proceed through a set sequence from values identification to the making of qualified decisions. Categories such as value identification and examination of consequences are useful for analytic purposes, but in real life they tend to overlap. As students identify their commitments, they are likely to start raising questions about the consequences of acting on them. Or examining the consequences of acting upon values may lead one to better insights about his or her commitments. In fact, a good way to involve students in value identification and clarification is to force them to confront the conflicts between the values in their own frames of reference. Another good tactic is to make them face the consequences of acting generally upon the values that are implicit in their classroom or playground behavior.

In short, a *logical* sequence for examining the components of moral values education moves from the identification of value commitments, through awareness of value conflict, to the confrontation of full-blown ethical problems. However, the greatest *psychological* effect may come from following a different sequence—one which first engages students in the consideration of ethical problems they can identify with, so that they become immersed emotionally. Then they can be helped to become aware of the difficulties in arriving at rationally defensible answers. The feelings of disequilibrium and the interest generated by this approach can motivate students to consider values and valuing systematically.

Finally, it is important to remember that values have a strong emotive (affective) component. Their emotive force helps to hold society together. But for you as a teacher, emotions can also be a source of

[5] A discussion of strategies for handling ethical decisions involving public issues can be found in Shaver and Larkins (1973a), *Decision-Making in a Democracy.*

contention. Administrators and parents may object when you try to teach students to handle loaded issues rationally. It is here that having a strong rationale, set in the context of a commitment to human dignity, can be a good survival strategy. Remember, too, that when students have been helped to develop the vocabulary and conceptual tools for value analysis, it is less likely that you will be accused of indoctrination—even when you do take stands on moral issues.

Current Events

Problem *Focus on the value of "fairness" as you read this section.*

A news item I read to my ninth-grade homeroom said that a white college student had been denied admission to law school because the institution had a "quota" system—a system that gave preferential admissions to minority students. The white student was suing the school because his qualifying entrance scores were higher than those of blacks who had gained admission.

"What's your reaction?" I asked.

Dick Simmons was grinning from ear to ear. "That white dude, he knows what it's like now! About time, too!"

"What do you mean?"

"Oh, you know, man! Step to the back of the bus and all that jive? So let the honky sweat it out—be good for him! Like maybe it'll build his *character,* you know?" Dick's voice was drawling and sarcastic.

I glanced around the room. Joanie Anderson's face was pink with anger. Her hand stabbed into the tense quiet Dick had created.

"Well, I don't think it's *fair,*" she blurted out. "I mean . . ."

"*Fair!*" Dick interrupted in a half-shout. He swung round in his desk. "You gonna talk about *fair* to me? Huh? You think Whitey was talking *fairness* and all that honky crap when they sent the slave ships over? You think working blacks on the plantations was *fair?* Or breaking up the families? Or white masters screwing the black women? You think being denied the right to vote was *fair?* Or segregated housing and restaurants and schools?" Dick let the questions hang and then drove in his point. "Hey, baby—you *owe* us—and you better get used to payin' up!"

Joe Sheridan didn't even bother to raise his hand. "Dick, you're full of it. Joanie don't owe you *nothing.* And neither do I. Nobody owes nobody—that's what I think."

Dick's sneer was cool and stylized. "Four hundred years, dig? That's what you owing blacks in this country!" His fist went up in the clenched symbol of black power. "Ain't no way you gonna turn back the clock!"

The challenge was unmistakable in Dick's voice. "That's true," I said. "Whites can't turn back the clock and neither can blacks. That's the terrible thing about our history. But it's also the great thing, too, because it shows us how far we've really come in the past few years."

"Blacks ain't been nowhere 'cept down the river," Dick said.

"I don't know," I shrugged. "I mean, look at this news clipping we've been discussing. Why, ten or fifteen years ago we couldn't have had this kind of talk."

Dick's eyes snapped with anger. "And you know why? 'Cause niggers hadn't learned how to play with matches yet!"

"You could have a point," I conceded. "Maybe that's what convinced *some* white politicians. But what about everyday people like Joanie and Joe? What about me? Do you think that burning down our places would encourage us to support the black movement?"

Dick fell silent as he chewed over my question for a moment. "Let's talk over this value of fairness," I added. "Maybe this kind of discussion can help us work things out for ourselves in the future."

Follow-up *Dick and the other students who entered into the discussion seem to have different meanings for the value of "fairness." Can you identify the various definitions—such as justice, equality of opportunity, retribution—and whom they fit? Which are basic democratic values?*

How would you work with this class to help them identify and clarify their commitments and relate them to basic value labels?

Story Within a Story

Problem *Notice how a classroom difficulty can provide the basis for value analysis.*

I looked over the scores on a science quiz I'd given my fifth graders and felt a twinge of anger. Once again there was that same strange pattern—a cluster of nearly identical scores from the back corner of the room.

"The honor system!" I thought to myself. We'd spent time at the beginning of the year talking it over, and the kids had agreed that they were "grown up" enough to handle the responsibility of taking tests without my constant supervision. Now some of them were apparently taking advantage of me.

I glanced at the classroom clock and wondered what to do. Throw out the test scores? Give the test over? Vent my anger in front of the class? Accuse the kids whose scores were suspicious? Announce that the honor system was going to be replaced by teacher monitoring?

I meditated on the alternatives for maybe a minute and then reached into my desk drawer for a ditto master. A narrative "springboard" for discussion was quickly scribbled out in longhand:

What Should Sue Do?

"C'mon, Sue," came the whisper. "Number four--please?"
Sue looked down at her paper. Her mouth felt dry and tight. She could feel the stare of her best friend, who wanted help on the test.
It isn't right, she thought to herself. It's cheating.
"Sue--c'mon! Number four."
Maybe just this once, Sue thought. For my best friend.
Sue hesitated and bit her lip.

By the time my kids were in from lunch I had run off enough copies to start the discussion.

"What do you think?" I asked. "What *should* Sue do?"

Almost immediately a hand went up. "Is it an honor system?" Scott wanted to know. "I mean, is the teacher around?"

"It's an honor system," I shrugged with a smile.

"Hmmmmmm," Connie murmured. "That's a hard one. It's really her *best* friend?"

"Her best friend," I answered.

"Maybe it would be okay just once," Mark volunteered.

"But it's *cheating*," countered Simone.

"Yeah, but just once—"

"If you do it once, they'll just keep asking you," Karen blurted out.

There was a lull as the kids mulled over what Karen had said. I decided not to pursue the cause-effect question she had raised, but instead to focus on the values—honesty and friendship—at stake here.

"On the one hand, Sue wants to be honest," I said. "But she wants to have friends, too. Let's hear from some other people. Don, what do you think Sue should do?"

Don's voice was little more than a whisper. "Uhmm, I don't know." He glanced up at me, then back to his ditto sheet.

"Well, this is a pretty hard problem," I said. "And it's one we all have to work out for ourselves sooner or later. You know, I wonder if it might help if we talked for a moment about these two terms, 'honesty' and 'friendship.' "

I went to the board and wrote down the terms for the value conflict. "Okay," I nodded. "Now, how can we figure out what Sue should do—and what *we* should do if we ever find ourselves in this situation?"

Hands started going up.

Follow-up *With somebody playing the teacher and several playing students, role-play the discussion that might follow. The "teacher" should attempt to get the "students" to define value terms, to examine the possible* *consequences of acting on one value or the other, and finally to state qualified decisions. After a few minutes of discussion, switch roles.*

Value Exploration 7

Reread "Inner Office Conference" on p. 80. Imagine that Miss Dunning has returned to class. One of her students says, "After all the work we've done, you still haven't told us where *you* stand on this water pollution thing."

"Yeah," another chimes in. "Don't you think it's about time for a strong water pollution law?"

The students wait for an answer.

Assume that Miss Dunning has acquainted her students with the terminology and processes of value analysis that we have discussed in this chapter. She decides that it *is* time to take a stand. Explore with others the kind of *qualified statement* she might make to avoid imposing her opinion on students. In doing this, assume first that she is in favor of water pollution legislation—then that she opposes it.

Pep Assembly

Problem *What values does Allison Hunt appear to be using to judge her pep assembly experience?*

Allison Hunt sidestepped her way to her official sentry position high on the right side of the new Wolverine grandstands. The stands were nearly full with noisy, colorfully dressed students. The sky was electric blue, the field an unreal green, carefully manicured for the evening's football contest.

Trumpets and blaring trombones crescendoed into the chorus of the school rally song as a small pack of sullen-looking black and Chicano youths straggled through the north gate, herded down the track by a beefy assistant principal. A squadron of paper airplanes sailed down from somewhere beneath the Dad's Club Press Box, looping gracefully over the heads of the Pep Club. Allison turned and tried to impale one whole section of the bleachers with her iciest teacher stare. As usual, this was met with uncomprehending grins and eyebrows arched in mock innocence.

Tightening her mouth, she turned back to the Rally Squad, which was going through a zippy new dance routine. She heard snickers and giggles behind her. Three black students were making a small show of bravado in their swaggering ascent of the concrete steps.

The problem, she thought with a sigh, was student disrespect—pure and simple. It was something you could feel—just in their attitude.

The grandstand exploded in an enormous bellowing cheer, and the rally girls down on the field went wild, their lithe bodies dancing and jerking like marionettes, orange-and-blue pompons spangling the autumn air with color. The noise came in waves. She could feel the release of tension built up during the past week in school.

The crowd quieted as the student body president smoothed his school sweater, leaned forward, and blew a quick test into the microphone at the fifty-yard line, where the players and coaches were lined up. It was time for the Pledge of Allegiance. Allison stiffened her small slim back and put her hand above her left breast as she had been taught to do. The air seemed to settle and tighten, and her throat flexed for the first words.

It was then she noticed that the whole section of black girls in the rows below her had remained seated. The first words of the Pledge began to echo through the grandstands. The girls were still sitting, erect, tight-lipped.

Staring at the Afro hair styles, Allison mumbled along with the rest of the crowd, feeling a surge of emotion. Her first impulse was to lean forward and demand that the girls participate. She repressed the impulse, suspecting that there'd only be some kind of ugly confrontation. There had already been one incident earlier in the fall when Chicano and black militants had tried to disrupt an assembly with raised fists and their own "anthem."

So now it's *this,* she thought. *Refusing* to participate—and denying their American heritage in the process. The surly attitude. Any excuse to draw attention to themselves and their "cause." So what did they want now? More concessions? A society without *any* kind of order and stability?

The pledge was finished, and the crowd sat down. Allison had an unmistakable bitterness in her mouth. As a teacher, she couldn't ignore what had happened today. Monday morning she intended to begin emphasizing some pretty important values in her classroom. But what approach to take . . . ?

Follow-up *Do you think Allison Hunt's concerns are legitimate? List the value judgments that Allison seemed to be making during the pep assembly. Then list the value or values underlying each. Check your lists against those of others who have read the vignette.*

Then consider each value. Would Allison be justified in trying to inculcate that value in her students? How about the value judgments? Would she be justified in trying to impose any of them on her students?

In light of the position on values presented in Chapter 6, how might she proceed to handle the problem in class—in social studies or any other curriculum area in which she may teach?

Two Other Approaches to Moral Values

Two approaches to values education—a "values clarification" and a "moral stages" approach—have been receiving particularly widespread attention among educators. Both appear to be more than passing fads, and you are likely to encounter them during your preservice teacher education or as a practicing teacher. In this chapter we review the two approaches briefly and make some critical comments. Our intent is not to suggest that either approach should be rejected out of hand. Rather, we want to illustrate the kinds of questions that a rationale like the one proposed in this book may lead you to ask when confronting new educational proposals.

Values Clarification

The names of Louis Raths and Sidney Simon have become associated with the "values clarification" approach outlined in their book *Values and Teaching* (Raths, Harmin, & Simon, 1966). Although the approach is applicable to moral values, its use is not restricted to them (see Harmin, Kirschenbaum, & Simon, 1973; Hawley, Simon, & Britton, 1973). In fact, the popularity of the approach in a variety of curriculum areas is probably due in part to its applicability to esthetic values, as well as to its emphasis on the personal concerns of students.

We believe that each person has to wrest his own values from the available array. . . . [V]alues that actually penetrate living in intelligent and consistent ways are not likely to come any other way. Thus it is the process of making such decisions that concerns us. "Instead of giving young people the impression that their task is to stand a dreary watch over the ancient values," says John Gardner (1964), "we should be telling them the grim but bracing truth that it is their task to recreate those values continuously in their own time."

—Louis Raths, Merrill Harmin, Sidney Simon. *Values and Teaching*, 1966.

The values clarification approach centers on the valuing process. It is concerned with techniques for stimulating students to think about and clarify their own values. Fundamentally, the strategy involves responding briefly to what the student says, usually on an individual basis, always without moralizing, and in such a way as to make the student reflect on his or her statement. The purpose is to set up situations that will encourage individuals to arrive at "values" themselves by considering their own decisions and becoming involved in "choosing, prizing, behaving" (Raths, Harmin, & Simon, 1966, Ch. 1 and 3).

Raths and his associates frequently use the term "value theory" in referring to their approach. However, little of what one might call a "theory" is spelled out, beyond a few assumptions underlying their basic approach. The major emphasis is on the types of activities that teachers can use to help students clarify values.

Values and Teaching discusses thirty types of clarifying responses that teachers might find useful (Raths, et al., 1966, pp. 55–56). Three chapters (Ch. 6, 7, and 8) are devoted to "additional techniques that teachers can use to get students involved in value-related discussions, thinking, and activities" (p. 82). In addition, a more recent book by Simon, Howe, and Kirschenbaum (1972) details seventy-nine more activities, or "strategies," for initiating discussion about values.

There is an assumption in the value theory and the teaching strategies that grow from it that humans *can* arrive at values by an intelligent process of choosing, prizing, and behaving.

—Louis Raths, Merrill Harmin, Sidney Simon. *Values and Teaching*, 1966.

There has been some research to determine the effects of the values clarification approach on students. According to Raths, Simon, and their associates, "the small amount of empirical research that has been done . . . and the large amount of practical experience . . . by thousands of teachers" (Simon, Howe, & Kirschenbaum, 1972, p. 20) indicate such positive results as students who are "less apathetic, less flighty, less conforming . . . less over-dissenting, . . . more zestful and energetic, more critical in their thinking, and . . . more likely to follow through on decisions." They also say that the approach has helped underachievers become more successful in school (Simon, Howe, & Kirschenbaum, 1972, pp. 20–21; also Raths, Harmin, & Simon, 1966, pp. 47–48, 205–229).

Some Reservations

Despite these claims and a frequently enthusiastic reception by teachers, there are some possible reservations about the Raths-Simon approach. These are worth raising because they have implications for the development and use of a rationale.

To begin with, Raths and Simon clearly do not deal with a decision-making *process,* but focus on one aspect—clarifying one's own commitments. You should consider this limited focus in the light of two other factors. One is the school's responsibility for the improvement of thinking. The other is the ways in which values are related to the decisions people make, especially in matters of ethics. Is such a narrow approach adequate for dealing with either concern? Obviously, our view of the moral valuing process includes much more than value clarification, although that is one important element in the process.

Defining "Value" Another serious reservation concerns the way these authors use the term "value," in contrast with our own definition given in Chapter 2. As we have already mentioned, Raths, Harmin, and Simon (1966) emphasize the *process* of valuing, and so define "value" in a special way:

> . . . [I]t would be well to reserve the term "value" for those individual beliefs, attitudes, activities, or feelings that satisfy the criteria of (1) having been freely chosen, (2) having been chosen from among alternatives, (3) having been chosen after due reflection, (4) having been prized and cherished, (5) having been publicly affirmed, (6) having been incorporated into actual behavior, and (7) having been repeated in one's life (p. 46).

This definition, with its behavioral emphasis, is discrepant from the definition of "value," and the consideration of the nature of values, that we have proposed as a productive basis for building a teaching rationale. You will recall that we defined a "value" as a standard or principle by which one judges worth.[1] We stressed that values are an inevitable and integral part of one's frame of reference, developing from and shaped by each person's experiences. And we noted that values are cognitive and affective (they involve concepts about which one has feelings). Finally, we pointed out that our attitudes are based partly on our values, and we also emphasized the

---

[1] See Chapter 2, p. 15.

distinction between the value judgments we make and the values that underlie those judgments.

From our point of view, if teachers adopt the Raths-Simon definition, there may be some unfortunate consequences. Their definition confounds "beliefs, attitudes, activities, and feelings" in a way that obscures the distinction between emotive and cognitive meanings, and so ignores the differing functions of each. The definition also fails to distinguish between value judgments and the principles underlying them. This distinction, we have suggested, is important to making and analyzing decisions.

Moreover, the definition ignores what is known about how our standards and principles develop. Often they are not "freely chosen" from among alternatives, after reflection, but are the unconscious result of our experience. By the same token, saying that values must be publicly affirmed is misleading. Everyone *must* have standards by which to make judgments—even though they may not have been publicly affirmed. To imply that some people lack values or may not develop them (Raths, Harmin, & Simon, 1966, e.g., pp. 42, 47, 194), which is a logical extension of the definition, is to deny this obvious fact. We could not function without values (as we have defined them), for consciously or unconsciously we are continuously applying standards and principles of worth as we make judgments. That individuals are not likely to have *explicated* their values is a legitimate matter for educational concern, as we indicated in Chapter 5. But it should not lead us to the erroneous conclusion that such persons lack values.

Values, then, may or may not have been "publicly confirmed" or "incorporated into actual behavior." Whether they are is often contingent upon opportunity. If a person has never had a given value tested, and so has never had a chance to act on it, we could not say that he or she lacked that value. We could only say that we lacked evidence as to whether the person had the value, and if so, how he or she would apply it given the opportunity.

Then, too, public confirmation of one value may run counter to one or more other values. Suppose, for example, that a high school student leader remains silent when American Indian students are denied the floor to protest during a Student Council Meeting. We might question whether she really has a commitment to freedom of speech (i.e., whether it is a value in her frame of reference). However, we could not conclude that she lacked the value—even if, to our knowledge, she had never acted on it publicly. Although our doubts about her commitment would gain strength if she consistently failed to support the value publicly, we should still be cautious about concluding that she lacked it. Even though she believes in freedom of speech, she may not see its relevance in the present case. Or she may be consciously choosing to support another value.

To summarize: Given a rationale which accepts value conflict as inevitable, it is not automatically a cause for consternation when a person fails to act in accord with his or her stated values. Nor does any particular action, or lack of action, deny the presence of unstated values. At the same time, as our discussion in Chapter 6 suggests, if a student consistently acts contrary to a stated value, especially one of the basic democratic values, the teacher not only can, but should, try to help him to clarify his reasons for doing so.

To always act consistently with all of one's values is impossible. To assume otherwise is to adopt a shallow and dangerous perspective from which to teach or to make other value-related decisions. A teacher with such a perspective will find it difficult to handle value conflicts realistically. Even worse, that teacher is likely to impose on students a value (consistency) and a value judgment (that one should always be consistent) that are unrealistic, and thus open the way for unwitting violations of values.

Which Values? In our rationale, not all value questions are properly the business of the school. In the area of esthetics, and with personal preferences and middle-level moral values, we believe you should be cautious about interjecting yourselves into a student's conscious or unconscious valuing process. Otherwise, you may open yourself to legitimate attacks by irate parents who object to interference in what they consider personal matters. Thinking carefully about your role as a teacher in a democratic society may help you to avoid such uncomfortable situations, and to defend yourself adequately if you are attacked (as we stressed in Chapter 4).

Interviewer: "Why do you say in the Introduction in the Handbook that in an area like relations between the sexes it's particularly unwise to encourage pupils to talk about personal experiences?"

Editor: "Because if you're in a group, the climate of a group which works together is very supportive in general. It's so supportive that people can be encouraged by this to talk about their personal lives in a way that they wouldn't like revealed to other people, and you can't guarantee confidentiality in the group. . . . When people talk in a group they can, unless they've been alerted to it, go farther then they would have wished when they reflect on it afterwards. Therefore they wish they hadn't said as much as they have said. It's quite clear also that there are cases where one person could be in a group and the other people who were involved in an experience or an incident, parents, . . . , somebody's girlfriend or boyfriend, is not in the group, and their private lives could be disclosed in a way they objected to. I think it's a matter of confidentiality really."

—Donald Hamingson (Editor). *Towards Judgement,* 1973.

Avoiding confrontations with parents is not the only reason, or even the most important reason, for being circumspect about inquiring into values other than basic democratic ones. Respect for the dignity of your students—

and, therefore, their privacy—should make you cautious about probing their beliefs and emotions.

Raths and Simon express little concern with the issue of which values a teacher should feel free to probe. They do discuss criteria for selecting topics "worth clarifying" (Raths, Harmin, & Simon, 1966, pp. 194–6), but they do not discuss, for example, whether a teacher should act with more restraint as value questions fall toward the personal end of the public-private issue dimension. We would raise such questions as: Shouldn't you be more reluctant to explore values having to do with private sexual behavior, on the one hand, than values having to do with racial discrimination, on the other?

Raths and Simon have produced many excellent, practical classroom suggestions for dealing with an essential aspect of valuing. In deciding how and when to use their approach, however, you should carefully consider questions like the ones raised above.[2] Such questions are, unfortunately, all too easy to ignore. How you handle them, or even whether you handle them, will depend implicitly on your frame of reference—unless you build and apply an explicit rationale.

"I want to be interviewed about *drugs*. . . . You know—like narcotics and that."

To examine potential tensions between value clarification and personal privacy, see "Jeremy and the Public Interview," p. 123.

Cognitive Development: Moral Stages

Raths and Simon's orientation is pragmatic. In contrast, the "moral stages" approach of Lawrence Kohlberg comes from a psychological theory of cognitive development that has implications for teaching. The theory is derived partly from the thought of John Dewey (Kohlberg, 1970a, 1971b, 1972a), but especially from Jean Piaget's seminal studies in cognitive development (see, e.g., Flavell, 1963). A brief consideration of Piaget's work is necessary to understand Kohlberg's position.

---

[2] For a more detailed critique of the values clarification approach, see Stewart (1975). We have been concerned with the lack of a rationale for the approach—a sort of non-intellectualism. Simon's (1975) response to Stewart suggests an anti-intellectualism as well.

Piaget and Cognitive Development

Piaget was trained, not as a psychologist, but as a naturalist and biologist (he published over twenty scientific papers on mollusks before he was twenty-one). As a biologist, he knew that organisms develop according to genetically determined patterns. Yet he found that when mollusks were moved from large lakes to small ponds, structural changes took place over several generations that could be explained only by the reduced wave action of the smaller bodies of water. From experiences such as these, Piaget concluded that development—both physical and mental—is the result of genetic maturation *and* adaptation to the environment (Wadsworth, 1971).

From Piaget's point of view, then, cognitive development takes place—frequently spontaneously and unintentionally—as the maturing mind carries out its intrinsic function of coping with the environment. The environment may be manipulated so that children will learn, but the development of thinking capacities is not due primarily to such manipulations.[3]

The significance of this view becomes particularly evident when it is contrasted with the long-standing emphasis on behaviorism in American educational psychology and the current stress on behavioral objectives and competency-based instruction. These movements identify the teacher's task as defining what students should learn and then devising the means to teach them. From Piaget's developmental view, however, the teacher's basic task is to set up circumstances to *facilitate* development which is more or less inevitable. (Put in terms of the moral valuing competencies we have emphasized in Chapter 6, the teacher's role is not to teach children to think, but to facilitate and refine the development of thinking that would take place to a large extent anyway as students interact with their environment.)

Piaget does not believe, however, that mental growth goes on helter-skelter, depending solely on the experiences that each individual happens to encounter. Mental development, he maintains, is also very much a product of the genetic structure of the brain. And because humans have similar organic structures, we can expect considerable uniformity in the mental development of different persons. In fact, Piaget proposes that predictable stages of cognitive development take place during certain periods of children's lives. (See Table 1.)

[3] Note that in this sense Piaget's view corresponds to the one we expressed in the discussion of education and schooling in Chapter 4. He too sees learning as a constant, inevitable life process, not something that happens only in school or when one is "taught"; and development is inevitable unless it is thwarted in some dramatic way (Elkind, 1970, p. 7–10).

Table 1   Piaget's Periods of Cognitive Development

Sensorimotor Period* (0–2 Years)

Stage 1 (0–1 months):   Reflex actions only.

Stage 2 (1–4 months):   Hand-mouth coordination.

Stage 3 (4–8 months):   Hand-eye coordination.

Stage 4 (8–12 months):   Means-ends behavior begins.
                          Absent objects take on permanence (child will
                          search for articles taken out of sight).

Stage 5 (12–18 months):   Child tries out different means (experiments) to
                          get what it wants.

Stage 6 (18–24 months):   External objects are represented in the mind;
                          symbols are used.
                          Child thinks out different means to get what it
                          wants.

Preoperational Period (2–7 Years)

Problems are solved through thinking about them.

Rapid language (2–4 years) and conceptual development takes place.

Thought and language are egocentric (they reflect the child's point of
view, not the views of others).

Orientation is perceptual (judgments are made in terms of how things look
to the child).

Imagined or apparent and real events are confused ("magical" thinking).

Attention tends to center on one thing at a time.

Concrete Operational Period (7–11 Years)

Reversability is attained (child understands, e.g., that the volume of liquid
is the same even if the shape of the container is changed).

Logical operations develop and are applied to concrete problems.

Complex verbal problems cannot be solved yet.

* Sometimes the word "era" is used instead of "period."

Formal Operations Period (11 – 15 Years)

All types of logical problems, including deductive hypothesis-testing, and complex verbal and hypothetical problems, can be solved.

Analysis of the validity of ways of reasoning becomes possible.

Formal thought is still egocentric in the sense that there is difficulty in squaring ideals with reality.

Source: Table adapted from Wadsworth (1971, pp. 114–115), and Kohlberg and Gilligan (1971, p. 1063).

It should be noted that the limits of the age ranges in Table 1 are not rigid. Although most children will tend to move through the stages at about the ages indicated, some will move sooner and some later. Also, a person may be at more than one stage of development at one time; so a youngster may vary in level of cognitive functioning from task to task and even from time to time.

Development is accumulative according to Piaget. That is, cognitive development proceeds in the order of the periods and stages of Table 1, and the child does not skip stages. Each period is the foundation for the one that follows; and moving from one to another involves important changes in the quality of thinking. So it is not just that older children *know more;* they *think differently.*

Another important point: It is to be expected that all "normal" children will achieve the concrete operations period, although perhaps not by age seven. However, some people never attain the formal operations level of reasoning. Some data (Kohlberg & Gilligan, 1971, p. 1065) suggest that this may be true of as many as 40 percent of the adults in our society. However, because they used small, limited samples of people (265 "lower-middle- and upper-middle-class" Californians) and of tasks (reasoning about the factors affecting the speed of a pendulum), this figure must be interpreted with caution.

Piaget's theory of cognitive development has many implications for teaching about values. Value Exploration 8, page 135, raises some questions to help you explore Piaget's relevance to values and teaching.

Kohlberg's Moral Stages

Building on Piaget's work, especially in moral development (Piaget, 1932), Lawrence Kohlberg has postulated three levels of moral development —the preconventional, conventional, and postconventional levels. Each level has two stages. The three levels and six stages are presented in Table 2.

Table 2   Kohlberg's Stages of Moral Development

Preconventional Level

Stage 1:   Punishment and obedience orientation (physical conse-quences determine what is good or bad)

Stage 2:   Instrumental relativist orientation (what satisfies one's own needs is good)

Conventional Level

Stage 3:   Interpersonal concordance or "good boy-nice girl" orientation (what pleases or helps others is good)

Stage 4:   "Law and order" orientation (maintaining the social order, doing one's duty is good)

Postconventional Level

Stage 5:   Social contract-legalistic orientation (values agreed upon by society, including individual rights and rules for consensus, determine what is right)

Stage 6:   Universal ethical-principle orientation (what is right is a matter of conscience in accord with universal principles)

Insight into the meanings of the stages can be obtained from Kohlberg's own summary (1972b, pp. 297–298) of the reasons people give for moral decisions. Note the differences in justification at the six different stages.

1. Obey rules to *avoid punishment.*

2. Conform to *obtain rewards,* have favors returned, and so on.

3. Conform to *avoid disapproval*, dislike by others.

4. Conform to *avoid censure* by legitimate authorities and *resultant guilt.*

5. Conform to *maintain the respect of the impartial spectator* judging *in terms of community welfare.*

6. Conform to *avoid self-condemnation* (italics ours).

Kohlberg's developmental schema clearly reflects Piaget's. As with Piaget's cognitive periods, Kohlberg assumes that movement through the moral stages is invariant. That is, development is in sequence from Stage 1 to Stage 6, and stages are not skipped. Also, as with Piaget's formal operations period, there is no guarantee that all persons will reach the highest stage of moral reasoning. In fact, it appears likely that a majority of people may not make it beyond Stage 4.

There is also a correspondence between Piaget's periods of cognitive development and Kohlberg's stages of moral development. Reaching certain intellectual levels is necessary before the moral stages can be attained. The major considerations are that the concrete operational period is a prerequisite to Stage 2, and the formal operational period must be reached before the child can move into Stage 3 moral reasoning (Kohlberg & Gilligan, 1971, p. 1072). However, reaching a logical period does not insure that moral development through the corresponding moral stages will occur. A person at the formal operations stage might still be at Stage 1 or Stage 2 morally. As with cognitive development from Piaget's point of view, moral development in Kohlberg's view depends not just on genetic maturation, but also on appropriate interaction between the individual's cognitive structure and the environment.

Kohlberg and Piaget agree, moreover, that teachers need to be aware of their students' stages of cognitive or moral development. Youngsters cannot handle problems that require thought at higher stages than they have attained. Problems more than one stage above their own level will be both incomprehensible and frustrating. However, teachers can encourage growth by presenting problems that require students to think at the stage immediately above their present one.

Kohlberg advocates this as a teaching strategy. Students not yet at Stage 6, for example, are presented with moral dilemma situations that they cannot readily handle at their current level of moral reasoning. Then, as they feel dissatisfied, the teacher must see to it that two things happen. Each student should listen to and be involved in arguments about the situations with other students who are at the next stage of reasoning. And the teacher should support the use of higher level arguments. Experimental evidence with small numbers of children suggests (Blatt & Kohlberg, 1973) that movement through the stages can be accelerated in this way.

Unlike Raths and Simon, whose approach emphasizes value neutrality, if not ethical relativity, Kohlberg clearly states that his moral stages involve "higher" moral reasoning. Reasoning becomes more complex as one moves through the stages, and morally better as well. His Stage 6 level of conscience-based decision making assumes a conception of justice based on Kant's categorical imperative (act as you would want everyone to act in the same situation) as a "basic and universal principle" (Kohlberg, 1970a, 1972a).

His own cross-cultural research in Malaysia, Taiwan, Mexico, and Turkey, as well as in the United States, has convinced Kohlberg (1968, 1971) that his stages are adequate world-wide descriptions of moral development. Variations in development are, he believes, due to differences in social context that push the members of some societies toward higher levels of reasoning than others.

To Kohlberg, then, the stages are universal in two senses. They describe moral development in all societies; and movement through them represents higher, morally better reasoning in all cultures.

Summary Kohlberg's Piagetian-based approach to moral development and moral education is clear. There are six stages of moral development. Children move developmentally through the stages in an invariant order, although instruction can hasten the process if the child who is cognitively ready is challenged to deal with moral issues at the next higher stage of reasoning. However, not everyone attains the highest stages.

The stages of moral development are also a hierarchy of moral justification. That is, each succeeding stage represents a morally better form of reasoning. Making a decision in terms of a universal value such as human dignity (Stage 6) is to Kohlberg patently better morally than making a decision in terms of a value such as avoidance of punishment (Stage 1)—and so, too, with the other stages.

Can you apply Kohlberg's moral stages to the reasons that students might give for their decisions? Value Exploration 7, page 115, gives you a chance to find out.

Some Reservations

Kohlberg's theory of moral stages is insightful and compelling, partly because it is rooted in the theories of Dewey and Piaget. Nevertheless, some scholars have their doubts about it. Some philosophers question the theory's philosophical base; others feel that it has not been adequately substantiated with fully reported research findings.

One area of concern has to do with the universality of Kohlberg's moral stages. You will recall that we proposed (in Chapter 3) that commitment to human dignity *might* be a universal value that could even serve as a context for international discourse. We did, however, suggest that as teachers we should hesitate to impose this Western, individualistic view on the world. Although Kohlberg apparently has no such reservations, there are those who question both his reliance on a Western, Kantian philosophical frame and the validity of his cross-cultural research methodology (Alston, 1971; Peters, 1971, 1975; Edel, 1974; Simpson, 1974). There is ample reason to be cautious about assuming that he has struck on *the* description of moral development for *all* people.

Serious questions have also been raised about the extent to which research with American samples supports Kohlberg's theory. Kurtines and Greif (1974) reviewed the research evidence available to support Kohlberg's theory of moral stages. They concluded that the results to date do not support his claim that individuals always develop through the same moral stages and in an invariant order. They also questioned research findings about the efficacy of "one stage higher" challenges in hastening the moral development of students.

Kurtines and Greif also questioned the lack of data supporting Kohlberg's claim that the Moral Judgment Scale really assesses stages of moral reasoning. (That is, they suggested a lack of evidence for the *validity* of the instrument developed by Kohlberg to measure moral development.) They also suggested that the lack of standardized procedures for administering the test makes it difficult to be certain that it is being applied consistently.

Teachers may have another reservation. Kohlberg's Moral Judgment Scale relies on one-to-one interviews in which moral dilemmas are presented in brief hypothetical cases and questions then raised about the proper behavior to handle the dilemmas. Appropriate paper-and-pencil, group-administered tests are not available. So not only is there some doubt about the accuracy of the test results, but the testing method itself is not practicable for the classroom.

It is also important to remember that Piaget and Kohlberg's developmental age ranges are averages that do not necessarily describe any given child. We can expect children generally to move into Piaget's concrete operational period at age seven; but some will not. A class of seven-year-olds, for example, will usually contain both preoperational and concrete operational children. The same is true of Kohlberg's moral stages. No class is likely to contain children all at the same stage. It may be expecting too much of a teacher to listen to a student's statement, judge the moral stage it reflects, and frame an appropriate "one stage higher" response during ongoing classroom discussions.[4]

---

[4] For a more extensive critique of the problems involved in applying Kohlberg's developmental theory to the classroom, see Rest (1974).

Implications

If there are so many serious reservations about Kohlberg's theory, why have we devoted so much space to it? For two reasons. One is that his work has sparked a great deal of interest among psychologists and school people. And in fact, despite the charges of narrow perspective and the shaky undergirding evidence, some educators are advocating Kohlberg's theory as a basis for "moral education." Some are involved in training teachers to conduct "moral reasoning discussions" to stimulate students to move through the moral stages.[5] The second reason is that Kohlberg's work does have some points of contact with the rationale we have been proposing in this book. We want to examine these to illustrate again the important implications that rationale building can have.

Kohlberg's position and the one set forth in this book both emphasize the importance of having students deal with problems that are real to them—that is, problems that are appropriate to the students' level of development—so that they can conceptualize, interpret, and become morally involved. Both positions also emphasize the importance of having children deal with value conflict—but for different reasons. Kohlberg sees engaging children in conflict as a means of helping them move to the next higher moral reasoning stage. We see value conflict as inevitable in a pluralistic, democratic society, and so argue that children must confront it in order to develop conceptual schemata that are as powerful as possible for coping with reality. It is important to remember that the criteria a person uses in choosing between conflicting values may well be contingent upon that person's stage of moral reasoning.

Behavioristic psychology and psychoanalysis have always upheld the Philistine view that fine moral words are one thing and moral deeds another. Morally mature reasoning is quite a different matter, and does not really depend on "fine words". The man who understands justice is more likely to practice it.

In our studies, we have found that youths who understand justice act more justly, and the man who understands justice helps create a moral climate which goes far beyond his immediate and personal acts. The universal society is the beneficiary.

—Lawrence Kohlberg. *Psychology Today*, 1968.

---

[5] Because Kohlberg assumes that each successive stage represents a higher level of moral reasoning, he recommends that teachers always encourage sub-Stage 6 students to move to the next stage. But is such movement always desirable? For instance, might not a democratic society be better off if persons who had the Stage 3, good boy-nice girl interpersonal orientation did not move to the law and order, respect for authority

Kohlberg's concern to date, then has been with cognitive development as a natural process that involves *changes in cognitive structure, not
the learning of any particular set of decision-making concepts.* The process
of development can, and does, take place without special awareness on the
part of the individual.

On the other hand, we have suggested that teachers should approach
values from a perspective of decision making—both on their own part as
educators and on the part of students as democratic citizens. Instructionally,
this means helping students become aware of how values relate to their
decisions—in much the same way as teachers should explicate their own
frames of reference and consciously relate their beliefs to their teaching
decisions. Values education in this context must include more than teaching
students to choose between values in conflict situations (see Chapter 6). And
even though the focus of this book is on values, we have suggested that if
conflict situations are to be dealt with adequately, students must be helped
to develop a decision-making model that helps them recognize and cope with
factual questions, language problems, and value choices.

An important difference in orientation is implied by the contrast
between Kohlberg's suggestions for discussions that may facilitate the
movement of students to higher cognitive structures and our advocacy of
teaching decisions based on the analysis of values and democracy. This
difference, we believe, is significant to your own consideration of a rationale.

Kohlberg has approached values education from the orientation of a
developmental psychologist concerned with studying "natural" stages of
development. We are concerned that teachers approach values from a more
comprehensive orientation. Kohlberg's instructional message is, "Here's
how you can facilitate the development of cognitive structure." [6] Our
message is broader: "Get clear on the assumptions from which you approach
the value-related decisions that permeate your teaching." One subset of
assumptions has to do with the cognitive performance that you can expect
from your students at different age levels. But other subsets have to do with
the nature of a democratic society, the teacher's role in such a society, and
the nature of values. These, we think, are more basic to the making of and
justification of teaching decisions than are the assumptions about development—although the latter should not be neglected either. Interestingly,
when Kohlberg has gone beyond describing development to making prescriptions about moral education, he too has had to become involved in the

---

orientation of Stage 4—if they are not likely to move on to Stage 5? That might even be an
implication drawn from the Watergate scandal. (This line of reasoning was suggested by
Donald W. Oliver during a private conversation.)

[6] We don't want to oversimplify Kohlberg's position by emphasizing his basic
developmental thrust. He is also concerned, for example, about the moral lessons of the
hidden curriculum (see, e.g., Kohlberg, 1970b).

"philosophical activity" of justifying his approach to morality (see, e.g., Kohlberg, 1970a, 1971a, 1971b).

There is another point of contact between Kohlberg's theory of moral stages and our rationale for dealing with values as a teacher. We have proposed that you construe your role as a teacher in the context of the basic commitments of a democratic society—and that, in moral education, you concentrate on helping students relate those basic principles to ethical decisions. Clearly, in Kohlberg's scheme, our position falls at Stage 5. It emphasizes the importance of making decisions in terms of basic values that the society accepts, implicitly and explicitly, because they are related to the central democratic ideal of human dignity.

As we have already noted, some data suggest that a large proportion of the population does not reach Piaget's formal operations stage, and that an even larger proportion fails to reach Kohlberg's Stages 5 and 6. Some people have argued that if it is frustrating—as Kohlberg suggests—for students to be confronted by moral reasoning more than one stage above their own level, then teaching decisions based on a Stage 5 rationale may be inappropriate, even counterproductive. We would argue that, on the contrary, one reason many people do *not* reach Stage 5 and 6 reasoning is that the school does not provide an environment that encourages moral development.

The principal told his high school students that they could not have a radical speaker because the speaker was against the government and the school was an agency of the government. If he had understood our constitutional system at the Stage 5 level, he would have recognized that the school as an agent of the government has a responsibility for communicating conceptions of individual rights which the government was created to maintain and serve. I am not arguing that the principal had a Stage 6 moral obligation to heroically defy an angry community of parents to see that a given radical speaker was heard. He was failing as a moral educator, however, if all he could transmit was Stage 4 moral messages to students many of whom were quite likely already at a Stage 5 level.

—Lawrence Kohlberg. "The Moral Atmosphere of the School," 1970.

Our response, we believe, is consistent with Kohlberg's admonition to the principal who rejected a radical speaker on Stage 4 grounds. That is, it is critical that values education in our schools reflect at least the basic constitutional frame of rights and responsibilities in our society, so as to encourage the development of moral reasoning to that level. At the same time, teachers should heed Kohlberg's caveat that confronting students with moral reasoning more than one stage above their own level may be dysfunctional.

Despite the reservations about Kohlberg's theory, then, you may find a knowledge of his stages, and of Piaget's periods of development, helpful. Even gross estimates of the cognitive and moral development of your students can help you to decide when and how to teach aspects of valuing and to avoid expecting too much from your classes. It may also help you to assist, or at least not to impair, your students' growth to Stage 6. Teachers who can tolerate, even encourage, Stage 6 thinking will be a welcome relief from the all-too-frequent fixation at lower moral stages manifested by those who deal with youth in our schools.

So even though Kohlberg's theory and our rationale differ in focus, they are to some extent complementary. The same is true of the Raths-Simon values clarification approach. Despite the questions we have raised, it should be clear that we see the clarification of values as a critical part of the formal curriculum. In short, our intent has not been to "put down" the values clarification or the moral stages approach. Rather, we have hoped to familiarize you with two current schools of thought and some criticisms of them. And we have tried to illustrate how a rationale can lead one to raise questions about *any* proposals for dealing with values in the classroom—including our own.

Jeremy and the Public Interview

Problem *Which is more important: Clarifying values or protecting the privacy of an individual student?*

"One more, one more!" the kids were chanting. "C'mon, just one! Please?"

"I don't know," I said. "I don't think so."

The clamor intensified. Any second now I expected my cooperating teacher in the next pod to come bursting in to bring the class back to order.

"Okay, okay," I finally relented in a cowed whisper. "Just hold it down, huh?"

The tenth graders quieted, and I realized that I'd been holding my breath. Just like a runaway stagecoach, I thought to myself. Give the horses their head and they'll take you all over the countryside.

"Who'll do the 'public interview' next?" I asked.

"Jeremy's turn!" Liz shouted.

"Yeah, let Jeremy do it!" came another voice.

Jeremy bounded up front and took a round of applause from his audience. I reviewed the rules of the strategy for him: He could either choose the topic or have me suggest one; after we got started he could "pass" on any question he didn't want to answer; and he could terminate the interview whenever he wanted. My job, as teacher, would be to ask questions and make clarifying responses.

"I want to be interviewed about *drugs*," Jeremy said in a cool, worldly way. "You know—like narcotics and that."

The class began hooting and giggling. "Okay," I nodded. "Would you like to tell us what you think about drugs?"

"Yeah. Like there's a lot of it going down at this school." He grinned at a buddy.

"You think it's a problem, then?"

"Yeah, you could say that. I mean, you start fooling around with some of that junk and it scrambles the circuitry upstairs."

"Well, how many kids do you think are using drugs regularly as opposed to experimentally?"

"Some of both." Jeremy winked. "But mostly just messing around. I guess. Like, you know, grass and pills—stuff like that."

"What's behind this experimentation?"

Jeremy hesitated and his mood seemed to grow a shade quieter. "I don't know," he said slowly. "Something to do, I guess—just being in with the guys. Or maybe just to see what's it like. Or to get back at your old man and old lady. There could be a hundred different reasons."

"That makes sense."

"I mean, maybe you're at this party and somebody starts a joint moving around. It's pretty hard to pass it up when everybody's watching."

"So it starts innocently enough," I said. "But—

"But then they *expect* you to smoke after that," Jeremy said. "Whether you want to or not."

My throat was dry and tense. "That could be a pretty tough problem," I said.

"Yeah."

"I'm not entirely sure of your attitude toward drugs," I said. "On the one hand, you seem to take a kind of cavalier attitude. But you also seem to regard the drug scene as a really serious problem—"

"Well, some of that stuff can really screw up your head," Jeremy interrupted. "I mean, so you can't think straight, you know?" The classroom was utterly quiet.

"We're running short of time," I said. "Maybe we'd better wind this up."

"I remember this one time that me and Andy Elliott and some other guys—Cleaver and Butch—"

"Jeremy, I'd like to conclude this interview."

"Cleaver was really flipped out. I mean, like it was *really* a bad trip. Anyhow, the awful part was—"

Dave Cleaver lunged out of his desk and through the open classroom door. The sound of his running echoed down the hall.

Follow-up *Certainly not all value clarification episodes end in this traumatic way. We have selected an extreme example to raise questions in your mind such as the following: (1) What topics, when used in value clarification exercises, are particularly likely to lead to violations of personal privacy? (2) Can you identify any criteria based on* your *rationale that would assist you in selecting appropriate topics for value clarification? (3) What sorts of basic understanding should there be between teacher and class before engaging in value clarification work?*

Considering the specifics of this case: How would you have responded when Jeremy said he wanted to be interviewed about drugs? Is there any point in the story where you would have directed the discussion in a different way? If you were the teacher conducting the class, what would you do now about Dave Cleaver?

Value Exploration 8

In Chapter 6, we discussed several aspects of moral values education. Now we want to raise some questions about how your students' cognitive development might affect the ways you teach the various aspects of valuing. Table 1, page 124, should provide you with helpful guidelines in considering your answers.

Preoperational Children

If you are in early childhood education or elementary, which of the valuing aspects do you think can be dealt with at the two-to-seven-year age level? For example:

Are children in this age range likely to be using "fairness" as an implicit standard for judging behavior?

Could incidents on the playground and/or in the classroom be used to develop a concept of "fairness"?

Could children be helped to use labels such as "equality of opportunity" at this age level?

Can the term "value," as defined in this book, be meaningfully introduced to children at this age? Can it be illustrated by reference to the standards they use implicitly or explicitly in their play and work?

Concrete Operational Students

Using your own experiences with children in the seven-to-eleven age spread, and through discussions with others who may have had more experience, what can be done with values during this period? Can you identify problems of esthetics, instrumental values, and ethics that students at this age level deal with in their own lives (maybe by interviewing some students)? [7]

What do you think of the suggestion that the child's life is to a large extent a microcosm of the larger society, and that the value choices that occur "out there"—in regard to such matters as respecting the rights of others, relating to authority, allocating scarce resources, to name a few—occur in simplified form in the child's encounters in the home, at school, and on the street? If so, doesn't that suggest that these situations could be used as the basis for preparing the student to deal with values in broader, more abstract situations as he or she moves into the formal operations period?

Formal Operational Students

Remember that current findings suggest that perhaps as much as 40 percent of the population never reach the formal operations stage. Consider such questions as the following:

How much can you expect to accomplish in teaching rational valuing at this developmental level?

What do the differences between the concrete and formal operations stages suggest about why students vary in their enthusiasm for dealing with problems, such as social issues, on a nonpersonal level?

How can you use the student's own daily life experiences to help him relate to broader problems? For example, can students fruitfully examine the ways in which their encounters with the school principal are similar to adult encounters with government in regard to such values as due process of law, freedom of speech, the right to personal privacy? (See, for example, Knight, 1974.)

The multitude of considerations raised above might best be approached as a brainstorming effort shared by you with other readers of this book. In addition, you might find it helpful to have on hand a very readable

---

[7] You may want to examine materials prepared to engage students at this age level in the consideration of value conflicts through role-playing. See, for example, the book by F. R. Shaftel and G. Shaftel (1967), as well as their film strips (1970) and films (n.d.). You may also want to examine value conflict materials prepared by Lawrence Kohlberg and Robert Selman (1972–73).

discussion of Piaget's theory, such as Barry Wadsworth's (1971) *Piaget's Theory of Cognitive Development.*

After you've filled in the table, you may want to turn to page 139 to see how we think the reasons should be categorized. Any differences between your decisions and ours, or between your decisions and those of other people who do this value exploration, would be a good basis for a discussion to clarify your thinking about Kohlberg's and Piaget's theories.

Using the situations in other vignettes (for example, the decisions facing Miss Dunning in the Inner Office Conference and in Value Exploration 7), can you construct the reasoning for pro and con decisions that might be used at different moral stages? Trying to do so would be a good exercise to share with other readers of this book.

Value Exploration 9

Reread "Story Within a Story," page 113. Set forth in the following table are some reasons that children might give for their decisions about what Sue should do. Decide what stage of moral development each statement illustrates and the age range at which you would first expect such reasoning to occur (according to Piaget's periods of cognitive development).

Response (Sue should . . .)	Reason	Moral Stage	Age of First Occurrence
1. help	. . . because her classmate will take it out on her somehow (hit her, keep her out of friendship groups) if she doesn't.	1	2–7
2. not help	. . . because the rules of the school must be followed or who knows what will happen.		
3. help	. . . because her classmate will do something for her in return.		
4. not help	. . . because people agree that cheating is not good, and she feels an obligation to do what most people judge is right—partly to gain their respect.		

Response (Sue should . . .)	Reason	Moral Stage	Age of First Occurrence
5. help	. . . because the person asking for help comes from a poor family, must work, doesn't have enough time to study; and she'd surely lose the respect of other people if she didn't help such a person.		
6. not help	. . . because her friends (or more likely, teachers or parents) would think she was being bad.		
7. not help	. . . because the teacher will punish her if she gets caught.		
8. help	. . . because her friends won't think she's a good kid if she doesn't.		
9. help	. . . because the person asking help has worked hard, and she just wouldn't feel right not assisting someone who deserved a helping hand.		
10. not help	. . . because even though her classmates approve of cheating, she just couldn't live with herself if she helped someone else on a test.		
11. not help	. . . because she can't see how doing so will help herself at all.		
12. help	. . . because following the rules of her "gang" is very important, and giving help to anyone in trouble at school is one of those rules.		

Our Decisions

Example Number	Moral Stage	Age of Occurrence
1	1	2–7
2	4	11–15
3	2	7–11
4	5	11–15
5	5	11–15
6	3	11–15
7	1	2–7
8	3	11–15
9	6	11–15
10	6	11–15
11	2	7–11
12	4	11–15

School and Teacher

Overcoming "mindlessness" in American education is the central concern of this book.[1] We have laid out some of our thoughts and tried to get you to probe your thinking in order to build a rationale for value-related teaching decisions. In particular, we urge you to shape your rationale as a professional who is also an agent of a democratic society. We wish to focus now on another basic point: That as a teacher you are part of an institution, and the institutional programs and patterns of interaction have serious value implications.

We want to illustrate this point in three areas: Facilities and extraclass programs, the treatment of minority groups, and student rights. The purpose is to encourage you to think about the school's impact as an institution and about what you should, or should not, do about it. To do this, we need to consider the school's custodial role and the status of youth—both of which contribute to problems of meaningfulness ("relevance," if you will) and student responsibility.

Our plea, finally, is that the school be "democratized." The question we ask at the end of this chapter is: What will your role in the democratization be?

The Institution and Values

Program and Facilities

Some time during your career, you may find yourself in one of these situations: You are teaching in a school with a beautiful new gym, but some classes are relegated to a windowless basement storeroom. You are working

---

[1] Silberman (1970a, p. 379) uses the term "mindlessness" to refer to lack of "thought about purpose, and about the ways in which technique, content, and organization fulfill or alter purpose." This lack of thought, he says, is the problem with American education, more than "incompetence or indifference or venality." We agree.

in a classroom with one set of ancient textbooks, while the district budgets thousands of dollars for new uniforms and trips for the marching band. You see the school promote interscholastic athletics for boys, but little or no effort is made to develop interscholastic athletics for girls—or intramural programs that would benefit *all* students. You are forced to supervise a "detention room" so that your colleagues will have a "dumping ground" for kids who don't "pay attention" in class. Your lessons are repeatedly interrupted by PA announcements from the office. You watch the librarian lock up her sanctuary at 3:00 p.m. so that books will remain on the shelf, where they're "supposed" to be.

What values underlie such situations? What do they communicate to students about the values that are important to the school and the community? About which activities the school values most? Should these situations concern you as a teacher, lying as they do outside the classroom and beyond the realm of your day-by-day contacts with students?

Minority Groups and the School [2]

How about the claims made by many minority group members that white middle-class values have become institutionalized in our schools, and that the dominance of these values is detrimental to the self-esteem of minority students? Or that the school's unthinking acceptance of white middle-class values interferes with meaningful education and with the school's own attempts to comprehend and respond to minority students? Or that the common institutional stance runs counter to the basic assumption that diversity is vital to a democratic society?

The [minority] child has only few options for dealing with the negative evaluation that the school places on his parents, his dialect, and his behavior. He can reject his parents, dialect, and behavior (and himself to the extent his self-identity is tied up to them) or he can reject the school (and fall subject to the pressures and humiliations the school will bring to bear on him).

—G. P. Nimnicht and J. A. Johnson, Jr., editors. *Beyond "Compensatory Education,"* 1973.

In the book *Beyond "Compensatory Education,"* Nimnicht and Johnson (1973) pose these questions better than we can, as they argue that

---

[2] For some readers, the message of this section will be familiar. It is our experience, however, that despite the advances of recent years, ethnic problems are still very much present in our schools, and worth discussing.

"culturally different" does not mean "culturally deprived" or "defective." They see "compensatory education" as a pernicious form of ethnocentricity and social snobbishness, antidemocratic in its assumptions and results:

> The "cultural deprivation" model is basically a defect model—children who are "culturally deprived" are seen as defective and their homes and communities are seen as defective. It is unfortunate that those who subscribe to "cultural deprivation" generally seem to be unaware of the effects that such beliefs have upon the students who are supposedly "deprived." The dislike of the different . . . , implicitly evident in most facets of the school, obviously has detrimental effects upon the school experience of a minority group child whose family's life style varies from that valued in the school. Dialect, dress, and behavior are integral parts of each person; they cannot simply be abandoned (Clement & Johnson, pp. 24–25).

> Unfortunately, inaccurate assumptions about and evaluations of dialects and verbal habits that differ from those of the mainstream are manifested daily in the classroom. It is unreasonable to assume that children are unaware of these assessments and reactions. Undoubtedly, some children adopt strategies of withdrawal and rebellion to preserve their dignity (Clement & Johnson, pp. 16–17).

> Social-class differences will produce a discrepancy because the school values and rewards behaviors the "lower-class" child has not learned, but it does not recognize skills and abilities that are vital to his survival in his own environment. For example, some children from "lower-class" families may have learned to care for themselves and younger brothers and sisters; they may have learned to defend or fight for their rights and interests; they may have learned to share and cooperate; and they may have learned to live with hazards of city streets or to roam over the countryside. None of these skills turns up on measures of school aptitude or intelligence. . . . The fact that a child is learning to care for himself or to protect his rights, instead of learning colors, shapes, and forms or "correct" English, does not mean he is intellectually deprived. It simply means that he is learning different behaviors, some of which are probably more valuable to him in his life situations than those the school values. . . . [T]he school should recognize that children from different backgrounds bring different strengths to school. The school should also learn to respond to a child without attaching negative values to what he has or has not learned before he comes to school.

The schools' ability to respond to children from culturally and ethnically different homes is affected by two interrelated problems. In general, members of the white middle class feel superior to members of the various ethnic groups; therefore, hostility and prejudice make the schools a nonresponsive environment. The fact that the schools have not developed the curriculum methods appropriate for different cultural and ethnic groups also makes the schools nonresponsive. Of course, the second problem of curriculum and methods is in part an outcome of the first. It is unreasonable to expect the schools to reform the society that created them, but it is not unreasonable for the schools to recognize their own limitations and to modify curriculum and procedures so as to become more responsive to minority groups (Nimnicht, Johnson, & Johnson, 1973, pp. 41–42).

Are such claims valid? If so, can you justifiably remain neutral in an institution that tends to judge students in terms of the values of one dominant ethnic-economic group, and uses the same frame of reference in interpreting the American Creed? Can you square an attitude of "noninvolvement" outside your own classroom with your conception of a professional educator?

The real problem for children outside the mainstream is . . . trying to cope with an institution which is based on somewhat different values, uses a somewhat different language, and has a negative opinion of their life style, their parents, their community, and themselves. The real problem for teachers lies not in providing watered-down work or in coping with children who seem hard to control, but rather in the difficult task of learning different communication and motivation systems—learning to respond to unfamiliar perspectives and experiences instead of repressing them. The real problem for educational planners and decision-makers is not to devise remedial "help-them-to-be-like-us" programs, but rather to broaden the educational institution so that it can adequately accommodate and respond to students from a variety of cultural backgrounds and life styles.

—D. C. Clement and P. A. Johnson. *Beyond "Compensatory Education,"* 1973.

Students' Rights

To turn to another value-laden area—students' rights—consider the following examples from Silberman's (1970b) study of American schools:

Item: A high school senior—eighth in a class of 779, active in a host of extracurricular activities (student marshals, General Organization, Key Club, after-school tutoring program, president of the Debate Society, among others), and described on the school's records as "intelligent, highly motivated, and mature," with "excellent leadership and academic potentials"—is barred from the school's chapter of the National Honor Society on the grounds of poor character. At an open meeting of school board candidates the preceding spring, he had politely asked a question which implied some criticism of the high school. In the opinion of eight of the Honor Society's fifteen faculty advisers, none of whom had been present at the meeting in question, none of whom had ever met the boy in question, criticism of the high school is equivalent to disloyalty, and disloyalty constitutes bad character. The seven faculty advisers who do know the youngster fight for his admission but are overruled.

Item: (from the Montgomery County, Maryland, Student Alliance Report): In the way of a few examples: one student who insisted that he would protest against the Vietnam War in front of the school was told by a vice-principal that if the student persisted the school official would see to it that he could not get into college. . . . Another high school student, a National Merit Scholarship Finalist, as it happened, was told by his counselor that he would get a bad recommendation for college because he was a 'nihilist.' He had been arguing with her over the values of the county school system.

More recently, the following item was reported in a Utah paper (*Logan Herald Journal*, February 28, 1974, p. 3):

PRICE, Utah (UPI)—Judge Edward Sheya Wednesday threw out the Carbon County School District's dress code, saying it violated the rights of students.

Sheya voided two sections of the code dealing with the length of boys' hair and the wearing of slacks by girls.

He also ordered the district to reinstate the original grades earned by students who had protested the code. *The district had lowered the grades as punishment for the protests* [italics ours].

Are incidents like these uncommon? We suspect not. Should incidents like these in your school district be of concern to you? How about the frames of reference of other school people when they lead to such occurrences? Should you ignore or tolerate them?

Leadership from the Courts

We have raised many questions; you will need to work out the answers yourself. It is worth noting, however, that on some issues—particularly minority rights and student rights—the courts are providing guidelines for school people. For example, courts have said that in San Francisco the school district must provide special language programs for non-English-speaking Chinese students (*Lau v. Nichols*, 1974), and that school districts must make special efforts to obtain certification for Spanish-speaking teachers to teach Spanish-speaking students (*Serna v. Portales Municipal Schools*, 1972). The use of achievement or "intelligence" tests with strong

Anglo middle-class biases to classify black or bilingual Spanish-American students as mentally retarded has been sharply attacked by the courts in recent years, as have ability-grouping or tracking systems that are in fact based on cultural-ethnic differences (McClung, 1973).[3]

Court decisions on the validity of hair and dress standards have not been uniform from one jurisdiction to another, and the U.S. Supreme Court has chosen not to rule on the matter. However, the Court has taken clear stands on the basic constitutional rights of students. In *Goss v. Lopez* (1975), the Court held that students have the right to at least "minimum" due process—a notice and an opportunity for a hearing—before being suspended from school for disciplinary reasons.

Another landmark case, *Tinker v. Des Moines* (1969), raised the issue of the legitimacy of suspending students for wearing black armbands to school to protest our nation's involvement in the Vietnam War. The justices of the Supreme Court were mindful of "the need for affirming the comprehensive authority of the States and of school officials, consistent with fundamental safeguards, to prescribe and control conduct in the schools," to insure "appropriate discipline" in order to avoid disruptions that "would substantially interfere with the work of the school or impinge upon the rights of other students." Yet in ruling that, in this case, there was not sufficient evidence to justify limiting freedom of expression, the Court made the following point:

> It can hardly be argued that either students or teachers shed their constitutional rights to freedom of speech or expression at the schoolhouse gate.
>
> Students in school as well as out of school are "persons" under our Constitution. They are possessed of fundamental rights which the State must respect, just as they themselves must respect their obligations to the State.

It seems ironic, at best, that the courts have had to tell the schools, the educational institutions for a democratic society, that students do not lose their basic rights by school attendance. Such rulings are significant in terms of the supposed goals of education. Again the Supreme Court speaks, this time in *West Virginia State Board of Education v. Barnette* (1943):

> [Boards of Education] have, of course, important, delicate, and highly discretionary functions, but none that they may not perform within the limits of the Bill of Rights. That they are educating the young for

[3] For teachers interested in following court decisions on such matters, the journal *Inequality in Education* is an excellent source—both its articles and its Notes and Commentary section. It is published by the Harvard Center for Law and Education, 61 Kirkland St., Cambridge, MA 02138.

citizenship is reason for scrupulous protection of Constitutional freedoms of the individual, if we are not to strangle the free mind at its source and teach youth to discount important principles of our government as mere platitudes.

The courts, then, have had to remind school people not only that students do not lose their rights by school attendance, but even that schools have an important educational role to play as models of democratic ideals.

HOUSTON (UPI)—An elementary school suspended five-year-old Billy Epperson from kindergarten because his hair is too long, despite pleas from his parents that the lengthy hair hides a birth defect and saves him from the ridicule of other children. . . .

"The principal gave the parents quite a bit of leeway for the little boy," [School Superintendent] Watson said. "But his hair became very long over the collar. When they were asked to cut it, that's when the problem's [sic] arose."

The Pasadena school district long has had a rigid hair and dress code. At least 40 high school students were suspended Tuesday when they staged a walkout to protest enforcement of a rule forbidding female students from wearing skirts more than five inches above the knee.

Twenty-five girls were sent to detention hall Monday for wearing shorter skirts. Several of the suspended students scuffled with police on the parking lot of a nearby church during the walkout.

— *Logan Herald Journal*, March 7, 1974.

It is bad enough that the confusion of esthetic with moral values and fuzzymindedness about instrumental values have led to the unreasonable application of often foolish hair and dress standards. That the school, the society's formal educational institution, is so frequently autocratic and lacking in respect for students and teachers, denying their freedom of expression and their right to dissent, is appalling. What will your position as a teacher be on such matters? Will you be one who takes the silent route, forgetting that to do so is itself an affirmation of certain values?

As we said in Chapter 4, these are not easy questions to answer. In fact, the school is in a difficult situation. It is caught in conflict between values (such as freedom of expression and the order necessary for education) and between groups with conflicting frames of reference (such as students, on the one hand, and unsympathetic adult taxpayers, on the other). There is also another constraint on the school that is not often discussed openly. But it is worth a careful examination.

The School as Custodian[4]

The distinction between education and schooling discussed in Chapter 5 is pertinent here. Children often find elementary school interesting. Schooling at this level has a tremendous impact because it is a new phase of the children's lives—they leave home for long hours for the first time, and they are introduced to basic skills and concepts in reading, writing, and arithmetic that help them comprehend, cope with, and enjoy their worlds.

But all too soon and all too often the school becomes a detentional, custodial institution for the child. Attendance is mandatory and the captive student audience is often not at all convinced that the teachers and administrators care about what is meaningful to them. Most of us—students included—are often reluctant to admit how little education takes place in school that could not take place elsewhere.

This is true partly because the school serves society as a solution to other than educational problems. Mandatory attendance is not based only, or perhaps even primarily, on the invaluable nature of the education students would miss if they did not attend. It is also based on the need to keep youngsters off the streets, out of their parents' and other adults' hair, and especially out of the job market. This "holding tank" function of the school is seldom acknowledged openly.

What comes close to incarceration for many students is an ever-present specter in the school. It lurks constantly behind students' antagonisms toward the school and its personnel. Because teachers have a captive audience, they do not always feel particularly compelled to be responsive to the students' wishes; after all, the students can't fire them. Yet teachers are also haunted with the knowledge that the "eager" youth they are teaching are often not eager at all—that they are decidedly reluctant, if not recalcitrant.

Who's an Adult?

The school's uncomfortable position reflects the society's ambivalence and lack of clarity about giving young people adult status. How can a modern urbanized technological society handle the transition from childhood

[4] To many students, the metaphor of school as prison would seem more appropriate. In many places, where schools are fenced, students can't leave the building or the campus during the school day, and movement within the building is highly restricted, the comparison indeed seems appropriate. We prefer the custodian metaphor because it is somewhat less emotively loaded and corresponds better to the way school people, especially administrators, often seem to view their roles.

to full adult status? How ought it do so? Such a society does not need its youth to make an early economic contribution. In fact, young people represent an unwelcome intrusion on the job market.

It is probably no coincidence that the vote was granted to eighteen-year-olds at a time when awareness on the part of the young was increasing at a rate that startled many older people. No doubt increased exposure through travel and television was in part the cause of the increased sense of moral responsibility and sense of self. And these were manifested in such phenomena as the hippie movement (which rejected an economically oriented life) and the protests against the Vietnam War (which were partly based on conscientious objections to killing innocent civilians).

Granting the vote is a gesture toward giving young people adult status. But while some societies have rituals—the killing of a wild beast, a slashing of the chest after a fortnight in the forest—to mark quickly and clearly the transformation from childhood to adulthood, our society still has no clear *rite de passage.*

Edgar Friedenberg's thesis in *The Vanishing Adolescent* is even more poignant today than it was in 1959. If we define adolescence as the time when the individual is searching for self-identity, then our young people no longer experience a clearly demarcated adolescent stage. Instead, they go through an extended period of ambiguity. Young people often have more maturity—in the sense of awareness and concern beyond themselves and the local community—than their parents do. Yet they are restless and impatient. Their exuberance and conviction are often frustrated by their feelings of impotence. Capable of constructive work, but without jobs, especially in suburban areas, young people are bound in relatively unproductive servitude to their parents while they mark time in school. They are all the more frustrated because it is hard for them to submit meekly and unthinkingly to authority.

This extended period in limbo between childhood and adulthood—so much of which is spent involuntarily, boringly, all too often painfully,[5] in society's "holding tank"—poses special problems for the school and its personnel. And if they fear young people or need to exert authority for personal satisfaction, administrators and teachers cannot deal with students in the open, respectful way the students want—and often demand. Thus the difficulty of the situation is compounded. It is no help when parents share the same fears and needs, and so take the school's side of the struggle out of a sympathy born of their own frustrating attempts to cope with young people.

The search for identity and its spin-offs occur now at much earlier ages than many older people can believe, trapped as they are by recollections

---

[5] Students who drop out are often in even worse straits, especially if they have difficulty finding a job. They are cut off from the youth culture that centers on the school's activities; and, although they have the youthfulness that the "adult" culture values, they lack the economic indicators of worth—and, therefore, the identity and self-respect—that come with employment.

of their own early years. The downward extension of adolescence is having an impact even in elementary school, especially in student demands that their school experiences be "meaningful"—or, in the jargon of education, "relevant."

Relevance

"Relevance" is undoubtedly a much overused word in pedagogical circles. Yet it conveys so much. The plain fact is that much of the curriculum has little to do with students' lives, either in content or in orientation. The notion that the subject matter and intellectual interests of academicians and teachers can, or should, be imposed on elementary and secondary school students should have received a concerted and vociferous challenge before now.[6] So should the pervasive but implicit assumption in our schools that knowledge—not necessarily even "good" knowledge, but textbook oversimplifications and overgeneralizations—is valuable for its own sake.

Actually it is rather recent news that students think the curriculum is worth attacking or even discussing. Many still do not. The action in school, let alone outside school, is someplace else. But, for some very astute young people—some loaded with A's and IQ and some not—the curriculum is clearly worth talking about, even fighting about. A lot of students are sick of the word "relevance" in talk about the school. Yet I have heard no student who is sick of the meaning of "relevance." As one boy said, "Something should happen in some class or course we're taking that has to do with *me*—what I'm thinking or feeling or worrying about or seeing in the world."

—Danforth Foundation and Ford Foundation, *The School and the Democratic Environment*, 1970.

In the 1970s, career education work-study programs have partly solved the problem of irrelevance. They help students to feel productive and are relevant to the world of work that will demand much of the students' adult time and energies. But such programs treat symptoms, not causes. Based on the premise that relevance is a matter of career orientation, they do little to help students solve the other personal problems they face or the social problems that they learn about via the media.

The problem of "relevance," of meaningful experiences, extends beyond the classroom. Students are rarely involved in important decisions about the curriculum. They are not on curriculum committees; they do not

[6] For one challenge, see Shaver and Oliver (1968).

attend faculty meetings; they are not responsibly involved in the decision-making, feedback process of course development. Nor are students usually allowed a meaningful part in the processes by which standards for school behavior are set and enforced, even though these decisions may have annoying to profound effects on their lives. Denying students the right to help decide school standards and policies is scandalous if one accepts the view—stated, for example, by the Supreme Court in the Barnette case—that the schools are obligated to prepare youth to be involved, intelligent decision makers. Student councils are notorious, almost laughable, for their Mickey Mouse nature. Only the shallowest issues are delegated to them, and their lack of real authority becomes obvious when they attempt to deal with any

FUNKY WINKERBEAN   By Tom Batiuk

Courtesy Field Newspaper Syndicate

issues outside the domain approved by the school administration. And school people wonder why students are often so concerned about rights, yet evidence little awareness that rights entail responsibilities. The custodial nature of the school lends itself to "doing for" students, rather than involving them in shared responsibilities.

Responsibility

Decision-making power and self-responsibility seem to us to be vital aspects of dignity. As long as teachers and administrators make and impose important school-related decisions, it is hardly realistic to insist that students be responsible. (The same applies at home, of course.) Not only do rights entail responsibilities, but responsibility presumes intellectual and interpersonal independence. That is, to be responsible, students must have the chance to make decisions about issues that matter, and the freedom to make mistakes and handle the consequences. Adults tend to overprotect youngsters (or at least to use fear of consequences as an excuse for not letting them make decisions) and thus deny them dignity. This is ironic, considering how often adults make bad decisions and have to live with the consequences—an error factor they rarely admit to their youthful subordinates.

The essential difficulty of schools in handling activities other than academic learning is the position of the child or youth within the school. He is a dependent, and the school is responsible for shepherding his development. Yet if youth is to develop in certain ways involving responsibility and decision-making, then the responsibility and dependency are in the wrong place. To reorganize a school in such a way that young persons have responsibility and authority appears extremely difficult, because such reorganization is incompatible with the basic custodial function of the school.

—Presidential Panel on Youth, *Report on Education Research*, 1973.

Democratizing the School

Our discussion of the custodial nature of the school and the status of young people and of the issues of relevance and responsibility, is intended as an argument that we need instructionally and administratively democratic schools—and that teachers should become involved in developing them. It is not a plea for the abdication of responsibility. Professional judgments must play an important role in curricular decisions, even when student concerns are given high priority and the relevance of the curriculum for youngsters is a basic consideration. Moreover, schools do need rules—guidelines for behavior—just as the "outside" society needs them for stability. Learning about living within a system of rules is certainly one desired outcome of schooling.

But these "givens" hardly justify autocracy or institutional tyranny. The rules should be developed (legislated) and applied (executed) in a context of dignity and respect. The forms for legislation and enforcement will probably not be the same for the school as they are for adult society—or for that matter, the same for the elementary school as they are for the high school—even if they are consciously shaped by democratic ideals. But to be democratic, almost all schools, and many classrooms, would need to change a good deal!

Clearly, our call to democratize the school is *not* a proposal for permissiveness. Any school reform based on the rationale sketched out in this book must be constrained by the recognition that value conflict is inevitable. Total freedom for youth in the school (or anywhere else) is not only unrealistic in terms of a functioning institution, but untenable in a context of opposing values. Rights must be balanced against rights. (For example, when does exercise of one student's rights to freedom of expression—through speech or other symbolic acts such as hair style or clothes—unduly interfere with another student's right to an orderly, productive educational atmosphere?) And of course, rights must be balanced against responsibility, an important value itself.[7]

How about You?

Teachers are often viewed as "professionals," responsible individually, or occasionally as part of a team, for making and carrying out instructional decisions within a broad framework of curriculum guidelines and materials provided by the district. It makes sense from that point of view to suggest that whether the school is a democratic institution largely depends on the teachers' classroom and out-of-classroom contacts with students. The preceding chapters have raised a number of related questions that we hope you will ask yourself as you make teaching decisions:

Have you explicated the value assumptions underlying your formal and hidden curricula? Have you examined them for consistency with the commitments of a democratic society?

Do you involve students in curriculum decisions in a meaningful way? Or do you use student involvement as a facade for carrying out decisions already made?

Do you see your role as responding to your students' concerns? Or are you so concerned with the integrity of your subject field that you tend to overlook the students' world?

Do you allow and assist students to deal with issues that concern them? Do you help them to develop the conceptual capabilities, including those in the area of valuing, that will better enable them to make decisions and function as adult citizens?

Do you fundamentally respect students—trite as it may sound—regardless of age, ethnic background, sex, religion?

This chapter also asks whether you should limit your concern to your own contacts with students. Each teacher, we have said, is irrevocably

[7] For an excellent treatment of the value issues involved in students' rights, see Richard Knight, *Student's Rights: Issues in Constitutional Freedoms* (1974). This booklet will be especially helpful to teachers who wish to explore such issues in their classrooms. Also see Cuban (1972).

a part of the institution of the school. And that institution does deny dignity to students in many ways: by unexamined value judgments that are manifested in physical facilities and programs (the frequent failure to provide interscholastic sports for girls is a case in point); by operating from values—in making curricular decisions and judging learning potential—that embody and imply negative views of minority group members; by autocratic stances (sometimes based on the confusion of esthetic and instrumental values with moral ones) that deny dignity to the young, work against strengthening students' commitments to basic democratic values, and discourage student decision making.

A 21-month study by the Center [for Research and Education in American Liberties at Teachers College, Columbia University] has found that the majority of junior and senior high school students feel their schools are undemocratic. This situation, the study states, is perplexing to students who are told that the nation is democratic and needs citizen participation but who cannot participate in the decision making process at their schools. The dilemma fosters in these students a lack of commitment to the democratic process at least as far as participation is concerned, according to the center.

— *Report on Education Research*, October 28, 1970.

What is the individual teacher's responsibility for the institution of which he or she is a part, for its various denials of dignity and its failures to model democratic behavior? You can have an impact through your own transactions with students. But what stands should you take during your interactions with your colleagues? Your principal and other administrators? The school board, parents, and other members of the public? And should you try to get your students to analyze the school as an institution—and perhaps to change it? [8]

The answers are not easy. They involve serious questions of personal welfare and political strategy, especially if you stand alone.

A maxim of pluralistic democracy is that people belong to groups, and that groups influence governmental actions. Your local teachers' organization may be an appropriate place to seek action. Can it be moved from the typical concern with the economic interests of teachers (which are important) to concern with other vital matters? A teachers' organization might, for example, be influenced to push for certification and tenure criteria that take into account not only academic preparation, but also behavioral

---

[8] Involving students in the analysis of the school as a political institution is one goal of a project sponsored by the American Political Science Association, located at Indiana State University (Gillespie & Mehlinger, 1972).

repertoires and characteristics that lead to treating students with respect. Or your teachers' organization might be encouraged to take and support stands like the one taken by the American Federation of Teachers in 1970 (*New York Times*, Aug. 20, 1970):

> PITTSBURGH, Aug. 19—Longhairs won a victory here today when the American Federation of Teachers voted at its national convention to support a student's choice of his own "dress and grooming."
>
> More than 1,000 delegates of this 200,000-member labor organization went a step further and voiced support for a student's right to "freedom to petition, including the right to petition against public agencies, governing boards and school administrations" . . .
>
> The resolution stated that "democratization of the schools," which is supported in the federation's constitution, includes the right to peaceful dissent "without repression by administrators or teachers."
>
> The resolution declares that students should have the following:
>
> Freedom of speech and expression, including a choice of one's own dress and grooming, the wearing of buttons or emblems or the carrying of picket signs.
>
> Freedom of the press, including the right to publish or distribute literature on school grounds.
>
> Freedom of assembly and association, including the rights to join and to urge others to join any organization.

Conclusion

Our consideration of values in teaching has ranged from the hidden and formal curriculum, through the nature of values and of democracy and the implications for value-related teaching decisions, to the school as an institution and your potential role in revolutionizing it. We have tried to show why it is important to develop a rationale for dealing with value-related decisions as a teacher. And we have proposed some elements in such a rationale that we believe are especially valid for teachers in a democratic society.

It is always a great temptation to narrow one's area of responsibility. In teaching, for example, you will be tempted to define your professional responsibilities only in terms of your classroom interactions with students. But we seriously question whether such a narrow role is consistent with a commitment to human worth and dignity, and the belief that basic democratic values do not leave student or teacher "at the sidewalk leading to the school," as the U.S. Supreme Court has put it. As agent and professional in a democratic society, you are responsible for making school and schooling more responsive to basic democratic ideals. It is critical that you contemplate these responsibilities.

This chapter has imbedded in it a certain pessimism about current educational practice. Yet the basic spirit of this book is optimistic. We have faith in the power of rationality. We believe that if teachers examine the assumptions from which they teach, what they do about, and with, values will be more reasonable and humane. Their teaching behavior will be more consistent with deeply held and vitally important values. Our optimism is also based on our belief that teachers, individually and collectively, *can* have an impact on their schools—*can* make them more democratic and more meaningful for students. And of course, fundamental to our optimism is a confidence in the good intentions of most of those who go into teaching; for without that, all is lost.

Finally, we share some of the fatalism of an American Indian educator who, in supporting the emergence of colleges controlled by Indians and "flavored with their own cultural values" (*Chronicle of Higher Education*, 1974, p. 2), argued:

> Whether Indian control and Indian involvement in their own schools will erase or minimize the educational tragedies of the past remains to be seen. . . . but one thing is certain: they can't do any worse than what has been provided till now.

In many respects, there is only one way to go—and that is up. We are convinced that value-related teaching can be improved and that our society's basic values can be better applied in the schools. We think that the process will be enhanced by teachers whose rationales are consistent with the ideals of a democratic society and are based on an awareness of the nature of values. Finally, we believe that if *you* accept your professional responsibility to dispel the all-too-frequent mindlessness of American education, and to help democratize the school in which *you* teach, your career and the lives of those you touch will be more meaningful.

Bibliography

Alston, W.P., Comments on Kohlberg's "From Is to Ought," in *Cognitive Development and Epistemology*, ed. T. Mischel. New York: Academic Press, 1971, 269–84.

Beard, C.A., *The Nature of the Social Sciences*. New York: Charles Scribner's Sons, 1934.

Berlak, H. and T.R. Tomlinson, *People/Choices/Decisions*. New York: Random House, 1973.

Blatt, M. and L. Kohlberg, "The Effects of Classroom Moral Discussion Upon Children's Level of Moral Judgment," in *Moralization: The Cognitive Developmental Approach*, eds. L. Kohlberg and E. Turiel. New York: Holt, Rinehart and Winston, in preparation.

Bloom, B.S., ed., *Taxonomy of Educational Objectives: Cognitive Domain*. New York: Longmans, Green and Co., 1956.

Bolster, A.S., Jr., "History, Historians, and the Secondary School Curriculum," *Harvard Educational Review*, Vol. 32 (1962), 39–65.

Bronowski, J., *The Identity of Man*. Garden City, N.Y.: The Natural History Press, 1965.

Broudy, H.S., *Enlightened Cherishing: An Essay on Aesthetic Education*. Urbana, Illinois: University of Illinois Press, 1972.

The Chronicle of Higher Education, "Unhappy with White Man's Schools, Indians Beginning to Run Their Own," Vol. 8 (March 1974), 2.

Clement, D.C. and P.A. Johnson, "The Cultural Deprivation Perspective," in *Beyond "Compensatory Education": A New Approach to Educating*

Children, eds. G.P. Nimnicht and J.A. Johnson, Jr. San Francisco: Far West Laboratory for Educational Research and Development, 1973.

Combs, A.W., "Educational Accountability from a Humanistic Perspective," *Educational Researcher*, Vol. 2, No. 9 (1973), 19–21.

Coombs, J.R. and M.O. Meux, "Teaching Strategies for Value Analysis," in *Values Education: Rationale, Strategies, and Procedures*, 41st Yearbook, National Council for the Social Studies, ed. L.E. Metcalf. Washington, D.C.: National Council for the Social Studies, 1971.

Cuban, L., ed., *Youth as a Minority: An Anatomy of Student Rights*. Washington, D.C.: National Council for the Social Studies (1972).

Dahl, R.A., "Decision Making in a Democracy: The Role of the Supreme Court as a National Policy-maker," *Journal of Public Law*, Vol. 6 (1958), 279–95.

Danforth Foundation, the, and the Ford Foundation, *The School and the Democratic Environment*. New York: Columbia University Press, 1970.

Dewey, J., *Democracy and Education: An Introduction to the Philosophy of Education*. New York: Macmillan, 1916 (paperback, 1961).

Edel, Abraham, Personal correspondence, May 7, 1974.

Edel, M. and A. Edel, *Anthropology and Ethics*. Springfield, Illinois: Charles C Thomas, 1959.

Elkind, D., *Children and Adolescents: Interpretive Essays on Jean Piaget*. New York: Oxford University Press, 1970.

Fields, C.M., "Supreme Court Hears Arguments in Minority-Admissions Case," *The Chronicle of Higher Education*, Vol. 8, No. 22 (1974), 1, 8.

Flavell, J.H., *The Developmental Psychology of Jean Piaget*. Princeton, N.J.: D. Van Nostrand Co., 1963.

Forbes, J.D., Teaching Native American Values and Cultures, in *Teaching Ethnic Studies*, 43rd Yearbook, National Council for the Social Studies, ed. J.A. Banks. Washington, D.C.: National Council for the Social Studies, 1973.

Fraenkel, J.R., *Helping Students to Think and Value: Strategies for Teaching Social Studies*. Englewood Cliffs, N.J.: Prentice-Hall, 1973.

Frankena, W.K., *Ethics*. Englewood Cliffs, N.J.: Prentice-Hall, 1963.

Friedenberg, E.Z., *The Vanishing Adolescent*. New York: Dell, 1959.

Gibran, K., *The Prophet*. New York: Alfred A. Knopf, 1923.

Gillespie, J.A. and H.D. Mehlinger, "Teach about Politics in the Real World—the School," *Social Education*, Vol. 36 (1972), 598–644.

———— and J.J. Patrick, *Comparing Political Experiences.* Washington, D.C.: The American Political Science Association, 1974.

Glasser, W., *Schools Without Failure.* New York: Harper & Row, 1969.

Goss v. Lopez, 42 L.Ed. (2d.) 725 (1975).

Guralnik, D.B., ed., *Webster's New World Dictionary.* 2nd ed. New York: World, 1972.

Hamingson, D., ed., *Towards Judgement.* University of East Anglia, England: Centre for Applied Research in Education, 1973.

Harmin, M., Kirschenbaum, H., and S.B. Simon, *Clarifying Values through Subject Matter: Applications for the Classroom.* Minneapolis: Winston Press, 1973.

Hawley, R.C., Simon, S.B., and D.D. Britton, *Composition for Personal Growth: Values Clarification through Writing.* New York: Hart, 1973.

Himes, C., *Black on Black.* Garden City, N.Y.: Doubleday & Co., 1973.

Jensen, A.R., "How Much Can We Boost IQ and Scholastic Achievement?" *Harvard Educational Review,* Vol. 39 (1969), 1–123.

————, "The Differences are Real," *Psychology Today,* Vol. 7 (December 1973), 80–82, 84, 86.

King, M.L., Jr., *Stride toward Freedom: The Montgomery Story.* New York: Harper & Brothers, 1958 (paperback ed., 1964).

Kinsey, A., *Sexual Behavior in the Human Male.* Philadelphia: Saunders, 1948.

————, *Sexual Behavior in the Human Female.* Philadelphia: Saunders, 1953.

Knight, Richard S., *Students' Rights: Issues in Constitutional Freedoms.* Boston: Houghton Mifflin, 1974.

Kohlberg, L., "The Child as a Moral Philosopher," *Psychology Today,* Vol. 2, No. 4 (September 1968), 25–30.

————, "Education for Justice: A Modern Statement of the Platonic View," in *Moral Education,* eds. N.F. and T.R. Sizer. Cambridge, Mass.: Harvard University Press, 1970a.

————, "The Moral Atmosphere of the School," in *The Unstudied Curriculum,* ed. N. Overley. Washington, D.C.: The Association for Supervision and Curriculum Development, 1970b.

————, "From Is to Ought: How to Commit the Naturalistic Fallacy and Get Away with It in the Study of Moral Development," in *Cognitive*

Development and Epistemology, ed. T. Mischel. New York: Academic Press, 1971a.

Kohlberg, L., "Stages of Moral Development as a Basis for Moral Education," in *Moral Education: Interdisciplinary Approaches*, eds. C.M. Beck, B.S. Crittenden, and E.U. Sullivan. Toronto: University of Toronto Press, 1971b.

————, "A Cognitive-Developmental Approach to Moral Education," *The Humanist* (November-December 1972a), 13–16.

————, "Indoctrination versus Relativity in Value Education," *Zygon* (1972b), 285–310.

———— and C. Gilligan, "The Adolescent as a Philosopher: The Discovery of the Self in a Postconventional World," *Daedalus*, Vol. 100 (1971), 1051–85.

———— and R.L. Selman, *First Things: Values*. Pleasantville, N.Y.: Guidance Associates, 1972–73.

Krathwohl, D.R., Bloom, B.S., and B.B. Masia, *Taxonomy of Educational Objectives: Affective Domain*. New York: David McKay, 1964.

Kroll, J., "The Arts in America," *Newsweek*, Vol. 82 (December 24, 1973), 34–35.

Kurtines, W. and E.B. Greif, "The Development of Moral Thought: Review and Evaluation of Kohlberg's Approach," *Psychological Bulletin*, Vol. 81 (1974), 453–70.

Lau v. Nichols, 42. U.S. Law Wk. 4165 (1974).

Lavetelli, C.S., *Piaget's Theory Applied to an Early Childhood Curriculum*. Cambridge, Mass.: American Science and Engineering, Inc., 1970.

Massialas, B.G., Citizenship and Political Socialization, in *Encyclopedia of Educational Research*, 4th ed., ed. R.L. Ebel. London: Collier-Macmillan Limited, 1969.

McClung, M., "School Classification: Some Legal Approaches to Labels," *Inequality in Education*, Vol. 14 (1973), 17–37. Harvard University: Center for Law and Education.

Myrdal, G., *An American Dilemma*. New York: Harper & Brothers, 1944.

National Assessment of Educational Progress, *Citizenship: National Results*, Report No. 2. Washington, D.C.: U.S. Government Printing Office, 1970.

Newmann, F.M. and D.W. Oliver, *Clarifying Public Controversy: An Approach to Teaching Social Studies*. Boston: Little, Brown, 1970.

Nimnicht, G.P. and J.A. Johnson, Jr., eds., *Beyond "Compensatory Education": A New Approach to Educating Children*. San Francisco: Far West Laboratory for Educational Research and Development, 1973.

————, J.A. Johnson, Jr., and P.A. Johnson, "A more productive approach to education," in *Beyond "Compensatory Education": A New Approach to Educating Children*, eds. G.P. Nimnicht and J.A. Johnson, Jr. San Francisco: Far West Laboratory for Educational Research and Development, 1973.

Oliver, D.W., "Educating Citizens for Responsible Individualism," in *Citizenship and a Free Society: Education for the Future*. 30th Yearbook, National Council for the Social Studies, ed. F.R. Patterson. Washington, D.C.: National Council for the Social Studies, 1960.

———— and J.P. Shaver, *Teaching Public Issues in the High School*. Logan, Utah: Utah State University Press, 1974 (first published by Houghton Mifflin, 1966).

Orth, M., "Pop: Messiah Coming?" *Newsweek*, Vol. 82 (December 24, 1973), 47.

Peters, R.S., "Moral Development: A Plea for Pluralism," in *Cognitive Development and Epistemology*, ed. T. Mischel. New York: Academic Press, 1971.

————, "A Reply to Kohlberg: Why doesn't Lawrence Kohlberg do his homework?" *Phi Delta Kappan*, Vol. 56 (1975), 678.

Piaget, J., *The Moral Judgment of the Child*. London: Kegan Paul, Trench, Trubner & Co., Ltd., 1932.

Postman, N., "The Politics of Reading," *Harvard Educational Review*, Vol. 40 (1970), 244–52.

———— and C. Weingartner, "A Careful Guide to the School Squabble," *Psychology Today*, Vol. 7, No. 5 (1973), 76–86.

Raths, L.E., Harmin, M., and S.B. Simon, *Values and Teaching: Working with Values in the Classroom*. Columbus, Ohio: Charles E. Merrill, 1966.

Rescher, N., *Introduction to Value Theory*. Englewood Cliffs, N.J.: Prentice-Hall, 1969.

Rest, J., "Developmental Psychology as a Guide to Value Education: A Review of 'Kohlbergian' Programs," *Review of Educational Research*, Vol. 44, No. 2 (1974), 241–59.

Rice, B., "The High Cost of Thinking the Unthinkable," *Psychology Today*, Vol. 7, No. 7 (December 1973), 89–93.

Robinson, P.A., "The Case for Dr. Kinsey," *Atlantic Monthly*, Vol. 229 (May 1972), 99–100, 102.

Rokeach, M., *Beliefs, Attitudes, and Values*. San Francisco: Jossey-Bass, 1970.

————, "Long-range Experimental Modification of Values, Attitudes, and Behavior," *American Psychologist*, Vol. 26 (1971), 453–59.

————, *The Nature of Human Values*. New York: The Free Press, 1973.

Russell, G.K., "Vivisection and the True Aims of Biological Education," *American Biology Teacher*, Vol. 34 (1972), 254–57.

Schmidt, J., "A Christmas Call to Conscience: Do You Hear the Animals Crying?" *Family Weekly*, December 23, 1973.

Scriven, M., *Primary philosophy*. New York: McGraw-Hill, 1966.

————, "The Values of the Academy (Moral Issues for American Education and Educational Research Arising from the Jensen Case)," *Review of Educational Research*, Vol. 40 (1970), 541–49.

Serna v. Portales Municipal Schools, 351 F. Supp. 1279 (1972).

Shaftel, F.R. and G. Shaftel, Dimension Films. Los Angeles: Churchill Films, no date.

————, *Role-playing for Social Values: Decision-Making in the Social Studies*. Englewood Cliffs, N.J.: Prentice-Hall, 1967.

————, *Values in Action* (filmstrips). New York: Holt, Rinehart, & Winston, 1970.

Shaver, J.P. and H. Berlak, eds., *Democracy, Pluralism, and the Social Studies: Readings and Commentary*. Boston: Houghton Mifflin, 1968.

———— and A.G. Larkins, *The Analysis of Public Issues: Concepts, Materials, Research*. Report to the U.S. Office of Education, Project No. 6-2288. Logan, Utah: Bureau of Educational Research, 1969. ED 037 475.

————, *Decision-making in a Democracy*. Boston: Houghton Mifflin, 1973a.

————, *Instructor's Manual: The Analysis of Public Issues Program*. Boston: Houghton Mifflin, 1973b.

———— and D.W. Oliver, "The Structure of the Social Sciences and Citizenship Education," in *Democracy, Pluralism, and the Social Studies: Readings and Commentary*, eds. J.P. Shaver and H. Berlak. Boston: Houghton Mifflin, 1968.

Silberman, C.E., *Crisis in the Classroom*. New York: Random House, 1970a.

————, "Murder in the Schoolroom: How the Public Schools Kill Dreams and Mutilate Minds," *Atlantic Monthly*, Vol. 225 (June 1970b), 82–96.

Simon, S.B., "Sidney Simon's Response," *Phi Delta Kappan*, Vol. 56 (1975), 688.

————, L.W. Howe, and H. Kirschenbaum, *Values Clarification; A Handbook of Practical Strategies for Teachers and Students.* New York: Hart, 1972.

Simpson, E.L., "Moral Development Research: A Case Study of Scientific Cultural Bias," *Human Development*, Vol. 17 (1974), 81–106.

Simpson, G.G., "Notes on the Nature of Science by a Biologist," in *Notes on the Nature of Science.* New York: Harcourt, Brace, & World, 1962.

Stephens, J.M., *The Process of Schooling: A Psychological Examination.* New York: Holt, Rinehart and Winston, Inc., 1967.

Stewart, J.S., "Clarifying Values Clarification: A Critique," *Phi Delta Kappan*, Vol. 56 (1975), 684–88.

Strong, W.J., The Development and Exploratory Field Testing of Situational Materials for Pre-Service English Education. Unpublished Ph.D. dissertation. University of Illinois, 1973.

Tinker v. Des Moines Independent Community School District. 393 U.S. 503, 89 S. Ct. 733, 21 L. Ed. (2d.) 731 (1969).

Tovatt, A., E. Miller, D. Rice, and T. De Vries, *Rationale for a Sampler of Practices in Teaching Junior and Senior High School English.* Muncie, Indiana: Ball State University, 1965.

Wadsworth, B.J., *Piaget's Theory of Cognitive Development: An Introduction for Students of Psychology and Education.* New York: David McKay, 1971.

West Virginia State Board of Education v. Barnette. U.S. 624, 63 S.G. 1178, 87 L. Ed. 1628, 147 A.L.R. 674 (1943).

Winkler, K.J., "Shockley Finally Gets Chance to Speak to Campus Audience," *The Chronicle of Higher Education*, Vol. 8 (December 10, 1973), 1.

Zimmerman, P.D., "Films: Creative Chaos, *Newsweek*, Vol. 82 (December 24, 1973), 40.

Index

(Continued from page iv.)

Pages 68, 69, 70, excerpts from "A Careful Guide to the School Squabble" by Neil Postman and Charles Weingartner, published in *Psychology Today*, October 1973, used by permission of Dell Publishing.

Page 74, excerpt from "Educational Accountability for a Humanistic Perspective" by Arthur W. Combs, *Educational Researcher*, September 1973, Vol. 2, No. 9, p. 20 (from column 3), used by permission of the American Educational Research Association.

Page 86, excerpt from "Films: Creative Chaos" by Paul D. Zimmerman, published in *Newsweek*, December 1973, copyright Newsweek, Inc. 1973, reprinted by permission.

Pages 86, 87, excerpts from "Pop: Messiah Coming?" by Maureen Orth, published in *Newsweek*, December 1973, copyright Newsweek, Inc. 1973, reprinted by permission.

Page 87, excerpt from "The Arts in America" by Jack Kroll, published in *Newsweek*, December 1973, copyright Newsweek, Inc., 1973, reprinted by permission.

Page 92, excerpts from *Crisis in the Classroom* by Charles E. Silberman, copyright 1970, used by permission of the publisher, Random House, and of the William Morris Agency.

Page 110, excerpts from *The Prophet* by Kahlil Gibran, copyright 1923 by Kahlil Gilbran, renewal copyright 1951 by Administrators C.T.A. of Kahlil Gibran estate and Mary G. Gibran, published by Alfred A. Knopf, Inc., used by permission of the publisher.

Pages 117, 118, 119, excerpts from *Values and Teaching* by Louis E. Raths, Merrill Harmin, and Sidney Simon, copyright 1966 by Charles E. Merrill Books, Inc., used by permission of Charles E. Merrill Books, Inc.

Page 121, excerpt from *Towards Judgement* edited by Donald Hamingson of the University of East Anglia (England) Centre for Applied Research in Education, used by permission.

Page 130, excerpt from "The Child as a Moral Philosopher" by Lawrence Kohlberg, reprinted from *Psychology Today* Magazine, September 1968, copyright © 1968 Ziff-Davis Publishing Company. All rights reserved.

Page 132, excerpt from "The Moral Atmosphere of the School" by Lawrence Kohlberg, published by the Association for Supervision and Curriculum Development in N. Overly (editor), *The Unstudied Curriculum*, 1970, used by permission of the Association for Supervision and Curriculum Development.

Page 144, excerpts from "Murder in the Schoolroom: How the public schools kill dreams and mutilate minds" by Charles E. Silberman, published in *The Atlantic*, June 1970, copyright 1970 by Charles E. Silberman, used by permission of the William Morris Agency.

Page 145, excerpt from "Judge Throws out Dress Code," *The Herald Journal*, Logan, Utah, February 28, 1974, used by permission of United Press International.

Page 147, excerpt from "School Suspends Boy, 5—Long Hair," *The Herald Journal*, Logan, Utah, March 7, 1974, used by permission of United Press International.

Page 150, excerpt from "Voices Inside the Beleaguered School" by David Mallery, published by the Columbia University Press in *The School and the Democratic Environment*, copyright 1970 by the Ford Foundation, used by permission of the Columbia University Press.

Pages 152, 154, excerpts from *Report on Education Research*, October 28, 1970, and Sample Issue, by permission of the publisher, Capitol Publications, Inc., 2430 Pennsylvania Ave., N.W., Washington, D.C. 20037.

Page 155, excerpt from *The New York Times*, August 20, 1970. © 1970 by The New York Times Company. Reprinted by permission.